19e

LESSONS 1-25

Keyboarding Course

+ **Susie H. VanHuss**, Ph.D., Distinguished Professor Emeritus, University of South Carolina

+ **Connie M. Forde**, Ph.D., Mississippi State University

+ **Donna L. Woo**, Cypress College, California

+ **Vicki Robertson**, Southwest Tennessee Community College

SOUTH-WESTERN
CENGAGE Learning·

Australia · Brazil · Japan · Korea · Mexico · Singapore · Spain · United Kingdom · United States

SOUTH-WESTERN
CENGAGE Learning

Keyboarding Course
Lessons 1-25, Nineteenth Edition
Susie H. VanHuss, Connie M. Forde, Donna L. Woo, Vicki Robertson

SVP Global Product Management, Research, School & Professional: Frank Menchaca

Vice President/Editor-in-Chief: Karen Schmohe

Sr. Developmental Editors: Dave Lafferty, Karen Caldwell

Consultant: Catherine Skintik

Sr. Market Development Manager: Mark Linton

Sr. Content Project Manager: Martha Conway

Marketing Coordinator: Elizabeth Murphy

Sr. Media Editor: Mike Jackson

Sr. Editorial Assistant: Debra Roark

Technical Reviewers: Gayle Statman, Amy Cole

Manufacturing Planner: Charlene Taylor

Production Service: PreMediaGlobal

Sr. Art Director: Michelle Kunkler

Cover and Internal Designer: Imbue Design

Cover and Special Page Images:
© Luis Francisco Cordero/Shutterstock;
© Jezper/Shutterstock.com;
© Joe Belanger/Shutterstock.com;
© Kostsov/Shutterstock.com;
© 3d Brained/Shutterstock.com

Rights Acquisition Director: Audrey Pettengill

Rights Acquisitions Specialist, Text and Image: Deanna Ettinger

Permissions Researcher, Image and Text: PreMediaGlobal

For product information and technology assistance, contact us at
Cengage Learning Customer & Sales Support, 1-800-354-9706

For permission to use material from this text or product,
submit all requests online at **www.cengage.com/permissions**
Further permissions questions can be emailed to
permissionrequest@cengage.com

Keyboarding Pro Deluxe Online Illustrations: © Cengage Learning

Key reach images: © 2011 Cengage Learning, Cengage Learning/Bill Smith Group/Sam Kolich

Keyboard images: © Cengage Learning

Microsoft is a registered trademark of Microsoft Corporation in the U.S. and/or other countries.

The names of all products mentioned herein are used for identification purposes only and may be trademarks or registered trademarks of their respective owners. South-Western disclaims any affiliation, association, connection with, sponsorship, or endorsement by such owners.

ISBN-13: 978-1-133-58895-5

ISBN-10: 1-133-58895-6

South-Western
5191 Natorp Boulevard
Mason, OH 45040
USA

Cengage Learning is a leading provider of customized learning solutions with office locations around the globe, including Singapore, the United Kingdom, Australia, Mexico, Brazil, and Japan. Locate your local office at: **www.cengage.com/global**

Cengage Learning products are represented in Canada by Nelson Education, Ltd.

For your course and learning solutions, visit **www.cengage.com**

Purchase any of our products at your local college store or at our preferred online store **www.cengagebrain.com**

Printed in the United States of America
1 2 3 4 5 6 7 17 16 15 14 13

Contents

The Power of Keyboarding...Starts Here!

LEARN . . . DISCOVER

Touch Keyboarding

Communication Skills

Windows 8 Basics

Discover the POWER of *College Keyboarding, 19th edition* print and digital solutions.

College Keyboarding, 19e, combines easy-to-use tools with a proven track record of ensuring classroom and workplace success.

Keyboarding Pro DELUXE Online (KPDO) provides the tools to master document skills for use in school, career, and personal situations.

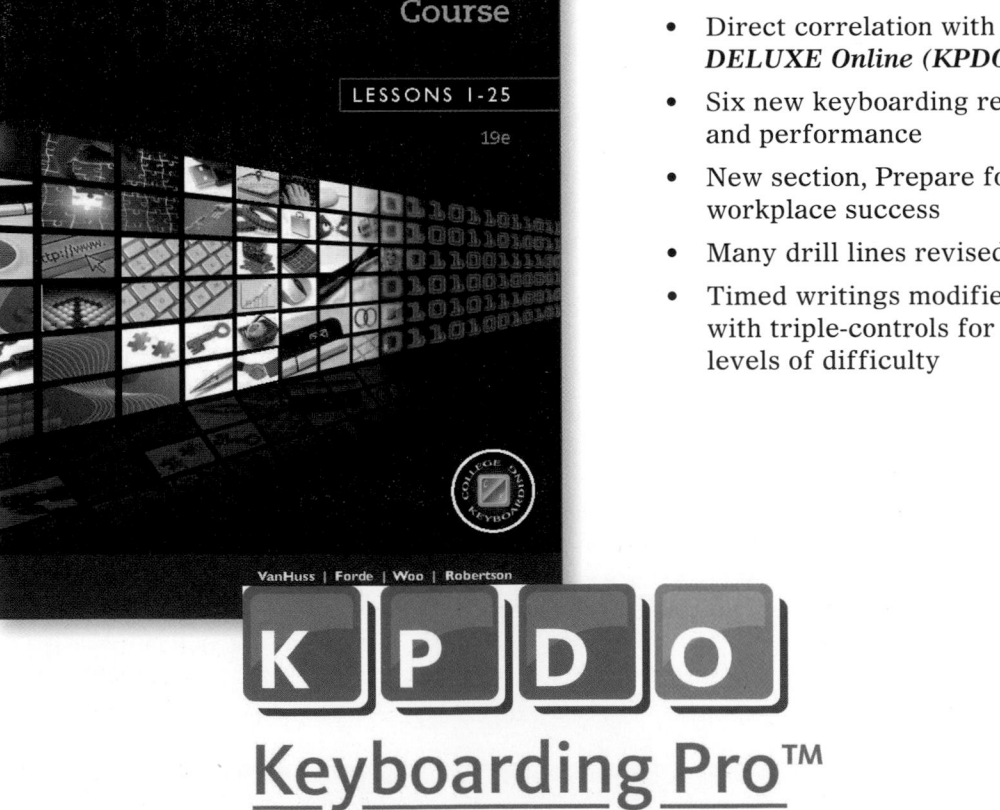

NEW to this Edition

- Coverage of *Windows 8*
- Direct correlation with the web-based ***Keyboarding Pro DELUXE Online (KPDO)*** to build, apply, and assess skills
- Six new keyboarding review lessons increase confidence and performance
- New section, Prepare for Your Future, shows the path for workplace success
- Many drill lines revised to emphasize basic skills
- Timed writings modified with triple-controls for levels of difficulty

The Power of Keyboarding... Starts Here!

Ready, Set, Key!

The keys to success include carefully designed lessons and reliable, dependable, easy-to-use technology tools.

An abundance of crafted exercises and a variety of relevant software routines keep lessons fun and help build a strong foundation.

 --Online and Better than Ever

Keyboarding Pro DELUXE Online (KPDO) is an easy-to-use web-based program designed to be used with *College Keyboarding 19e.*

- Textbook directions correlate with *KPDO*
- Relevant, engaging routines that work
- Abundance of Skill Building
- Meaningful, easy-to-use reports

| LESSONS | SKILL BUILDING | TIMED WRITINGS | REFERENCES | KEYPAD | GAMES | REPORTS |

Always Relevant, Fresh, and New

Extra Practice Builds Confidence and Success

Skill Builders in the text, Skill Building Drills in *KPDO*, Textbook Keying, and Timed Writings provide extra practice to strengthen accuracy and techniques.

Communication Skills Integrated

KPDO has related **Communications** activities.

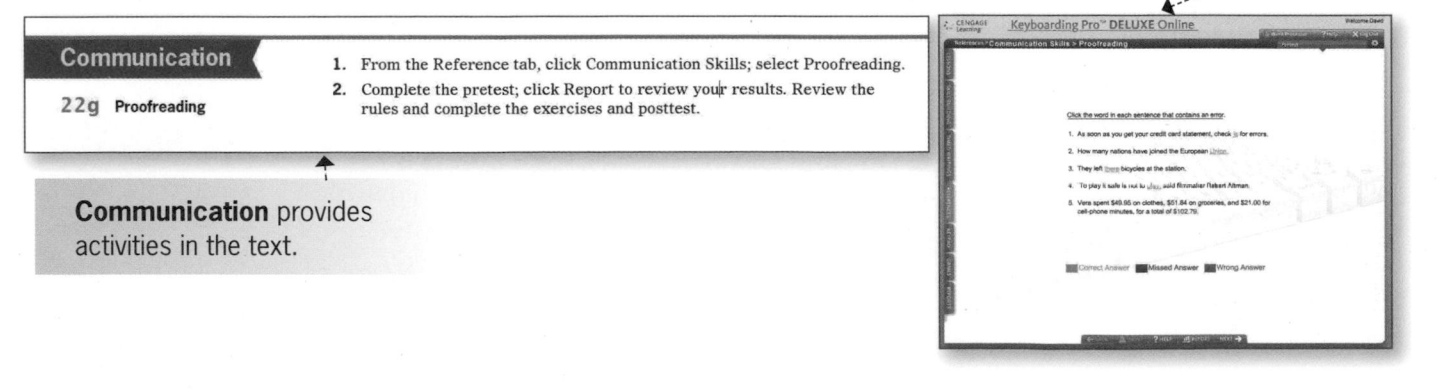

Communication	
22g Proofreading	1. From the Reference tab, click Communication Skills; select Proofreading.
	2. Complete the pretest; click Report to review your results. Review the rules and complete the exercises and posttest.

Communication provides activities in the text.

Powerful Tools . . . Working for You

College Keyboarding 19e provides the tools students need to develop expertise in keyboarding, document formatting, and essential word processing skills using *Microsoft Word 2013*. When coupled with *Keyboarding Pro DELUXE Online (KPDO)*, students can work at home or school with ease.

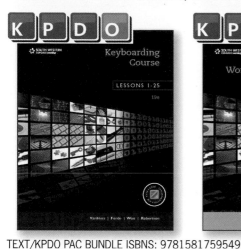 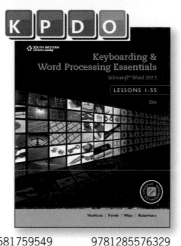  

TEXT/KPDO PAC BUNDLE ISBNS: 9781581759549   9781285576329   9781285576282   9781285576336

Keyboarding Pro DELUXE Online (KPDO)—Customizable

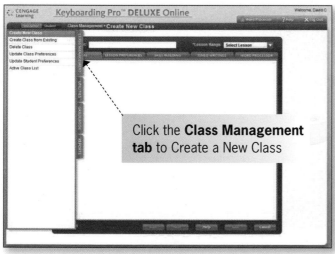

Click the **Class Management tab** to Create a New Class

Instructor Main Screen—Create New Class

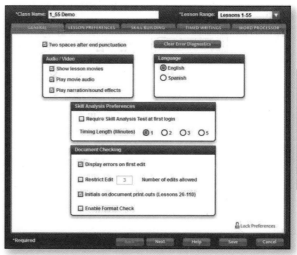

Set Preferences for general, lessons, skill building, timed writings, and the word processor

Set Class Preferences

◊ Customizable class preferences

◊ Gradebook to track progress on timed writings, daily assignments, tests, and more

◊ Quick toggle to student *Word* documents

◊ Reference tools for Communication Skills, Document Formats, and more

◊ Document checking of keystrokes with optional format checking

www.collegekeyboarding.com www.cengagebrain.com

New Content and Changes in Lessons 1–25

Level 1	New Content and Changes in Level 1 Front Matter

New section, entitled *KPDO . . . YOUR TOOLS FOR SUCCESS*, on how to use the new *Keyboarding Pro DELUXE Online* (*KPDO*).

Modules 1–2	Developing Keyboarding Skill, Lessons 1–25, Skill Builders 1 and 2

Six new review lessons were added–four lessons review alphabetic reaches in Module 1 and two lessons review numbers and symbols in Module 2.

Many drill lines were revised and keying tips placed above them to emphasize basic skills.

Modified and added timed writings triple-controlled at the easy level of difficulty in Module 1 and at the low-average level of difficulty in Module 2 to build confidence and gradually increase skill.

Materials are formatted using one space after colons and after periods to conform to current business usage.

Many exercises are repositioned to align them in the same sequence as *KPDO*.

Level 2	New Content and Changes in Level 2

Complete update to Word Processing using Windows 8 Word Processor.

Communications—Documents updated to *Word 2013* and several drills updated.

Web-Based Computing—Major revisions.

New six-page section—Preparing for Your Future (Career exploration and preparation activites).

	Reference Guide

Keyboarding—Bridge to Today's Technology updated.

New Windows 8 and File Management sections.

KPDO...Your Tool for Success

Welcome to *Keyboarding Pro DELUXE Online (KPDO)*, a web-based, easy-to-use, tutorial software for learning the alphabetic and number keys, numeric keypad, and document processing with *Word 2013*. You are about to tap into the best digital solution available for keyboarding and word processing instruction; enjoy and learn. The essential information about *KPDO* is covered below.

WHAT DO I NEED TO GET STARTED?

- Computer with high-speed Internet connection
- Firefox or Internet Explorer browser
- For a course in the Lesson 1–25 range, *Word 2013* is not required.
- A username and password for www.cengagebrain.com.
- Access code for *KPDO* that corresponds to the book you are using. You can purchase this at cengagebrain.com or through your bookstore.
- Course Code from your instructor.

INSTALLING THE *KPDO* TOOLS

The first time you access *KPDO*, the program will check your computer for various components to make sure your computer is configured to run the software. Depending on what is already installed on your computer, you may not have to install all the components. On subsequent log ins, the student portal will display as soon as you click the link from your bookshelf.

For step-by-step help with installing the program, go to the *KPDO* student companion site.

Microsoft Visual Studio Tools for Office Version 4

Flash Player

KPDO Plug-in

KPDO Word Add In

INSTRUCTIONS FOR LOGGING INTO *KPDO*

See page 2, steps 2 and 3.

WELCOME SCREEN

Read the Welcome screen to get a quick overview of the software. Return to the Welcome page by clicking the product name in gray. Use the **Skill Analysis** button at the bottom of the screen to test your current skill by taking the timed writing. If the Skill Analysis is required, you will not be able to go into the lessons until you take the timing. Key at a controlled pace that is comfortable and concentrate on keying accurately. Results display in the Skill Analysis report.

NAVIGATING *KPDO*

Left Navigation Bar

Lessons, Skill Building, Timed Writings, References, Keypad, Games, Reports— These tabs at the left side will take you to lessons and various activities. Tabs and menus display for each option. Once you make a selection, the left navigation menu closes so that you can view your activity in a full screen.

When you select a lesson, *KPDO* opens to the first activity. The other activities associated with that lesson appear in a drop-down menu at the right. This menu collapses; simply click it when you want to navigate between activities.

Top Navigation Bar

The top navigation bar lists your name and includes access to important features.

Word Processor—A *Windows* word processor that enables you to create documents or key drills and timed writings.

Log Out—Saves your work and closes your *KPDO* session and returns you to the Cengage dashboard. Log Out of the software each time you exit the program.

Preferences—You may be able to customize some preferences, depending on whether your instructor has locked them.

Bottom Navigation Bar

Some screens have buttons at the bottom of the screen. The buttons are specific to the screen you are viewing. They will enable/disable based upon your current activity.

TIMED WRITINGS

Timed Writings are keyed from the textbook. They appear in some lessons, and they are available from the Timed Writing tab. Results are reported on the Last 40 Timed Writings report. If the results meet the accuracy requirement set by your instructor, they appear on the Best Timed Writing Report. Error Diagnostics tracks the errors by row, finger, and type of reach on each timing. To improve accuracy on the type of reach you are making most frequently, see Drill Practice on the Skill Building tab. For best results when keying timed writings, focus on the words you are keying, keep calm, and concentrate.

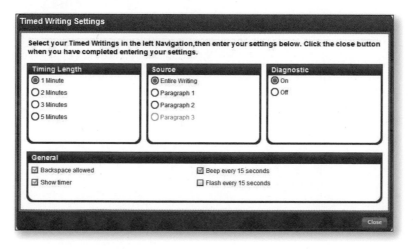

REFERENCES

The References tab includes tutorials to review Document formats, Communication Skills, and videos to reinforce posture.

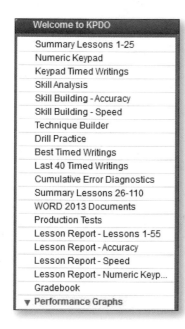

KEYPAD

The Keypad lessons and timed writings will help you build a strong foundation in 10-key skills. Extra Keypad Practice drills are in Appendix A of your textbook.

REPORTS

The Report tab shown at the left displays a variety of reports for reviewing your lesson results, skill building lessons and activities, and timed writings. Many of the reports hyperlink, giving greater detail; go ahead and dig deeper into the results.

Know Your Computer

The numbered parts are found on most computers. The location of some parts will vary.

1. **CPU (Central Processing Unit):** Internal operating unit or "brain" of computer.

2. **CD-ROM drive:** Reads data from and writes data to a CD or DVD.

3. **Monitor:** Displays text and graphics on a screen.

4. **Mouse:** Used to input commands.

5. **Keyboard:** An arrangement of letter, figure, symbol, control, function, and editing keys and a numeric keypad.

KEYBOARD ARRANGEMENT

Photos © 2010 Shutterstock.com. by permission.

1. **Alphanumeric keys:** Letters, numbers, and symbols.

2. **Numeric keypad:** Keys at the right side of the keyboard used to enter numeric copy and perform calculations.

3. **Function (F) keys:** Used to execute commands, sometimes with other keys. Commands vary with software.

4. **Arrow keys:** Move insertion point up, down, left, or right.

5. **ESC (Escape):** Closes a software menu or dialog box.

6. **TAB:** Moves the insertion point to a preset position.

7. **CAPS LOCK:** Used to make all capital letters.

8. **SHIFT:** Makes capital letters and symbols shown at tops of number keys.

9. **CTRL (Control):** With other key(s), executes commands. Commands may vary with software.

10. **ALT (Alternate):** With other key(s), executes commands. Commands may vary with software.

11. **Space Bar:** Inserts a space in text.

12. **ENTER (return):** Moves insertion point to margin and down to next line. Also used to execute commands.

13. **DELETE:** Removes text to the right of insertion point.

14. **NUM LOCK:** Activates/deactivates numeric keypad.

15. **INSERT:** Activates insert or typeover.

16. **BACKSPACE:** Deletes text to the left of insertion point.

Keyboarding—Foundation for All Careers

Learning Outcomes

Keyboarding

+ Key the alphabetic and numeric keys by touch.

+ Develop good keyboarding techniques.

+ Key fluently—at least 25 words per minute.

+ Develop reasonable accuracy.

Communication Skills

+ Develop proofreading skills.

+ Apply proofreaders' marks and revise text.

If you have a work schedule conflict, ask your instructor to approve your participation by telephone. All members must participate in the discussion.

Part III, Option 1 – Team Meeting and Discussion (Team Option)

1. Meet with your team and discuss the answers each of you obtained. If you are in the same location, use a face-to-face team meeting. If you are distance education students meeting in different locations, use a chat or discussion option.
2. List all soft skills recommended by the individuals interviewed.
3. Reach a consensus on what the team thinks are the five most important soft skills recommended by the individuals interviewed. (Do not vote—discuss until you agree on the important soft skills.)

Part III, Option 2 – Research Soft Skills (Individual Option)

1. Locate and find three current articles on soft skills needed most by employees. Make sure they come from reliable sources. Key the names and source information for the articles. Write a sentence or two on why you believe each source is reliable.
2. Compare the soft skills from your interview notes to those recommended in the three articles.
3. Prepare a list of at least 10 important soft skills from your interview and the articles.
4. Review them carefully and list the five soft skills that you think are most important for your career.

Part IV – Soft Skills Assessment (Required for Both Teams and Individuals)

1. Use a 1 to 5 scale with 5 being the highest (your strengths) and 1 being the lowest (your weaknesses) to evaluate yourself honestly on the five most important soft skills listed in Part III, Option 1 or 2.
2. List things that you can do to improve on the two skills that were rated lowest in item 1 above. Use the Internet to research this topic if necessary.

Part V – Team Assessment (Team Requirement)

1. Rate each member of your team and yourself on the following points using the same 1 to 5 scale that you used in Part IV. Key the team member's name and the rating on each of the five following evaluation questions:
   a. Did the team member share good interview notes from his or her interview?
   b. Did the team member meet the timeline provided by your instructor?
   c. Did the team member participate effectively in the discussion?
   d. Did the team member respect opinions of others and encourage all to share their thoughts?
   e. Did the team member do his or her fair share of the work?
2. For each team member, list the soft skills that were used most effectively during this activity.
3. In industry, leaders usually assess the results or outcomes produced by the whole team—not what each team member did. Would you be comfortable if the same standard were applied to your team—the same grade would be given to all team members? Why or why not?

Getting Started with KPDO

Step 1: What Do I Need to Get Started?

1. Computer with high-speed Internet connection and Firefox or Internet Explorer.
2. *Microsoft Word 2013* installed on your computer. If you are registering for a course in the Lesson 1-25 range only, *Word 2013* is not required.
3. A username and password for www.Cengagebrain.com.
4. Access code for *Keyboarding Pro DELUXE Online (KPDO)* that corresponds to the book you are using.
5. Course Code from your instructor.

Step 2: Register KPDO Using Your Access Code.

1. Go to http://login.cengagebrain.com. Enter your username and password and click Log In. Select Sign Up to create an account if you do not have one.
2. Add *KPDO* to your bookshelf by entering your access code, which may be in a packaged slimpack or an instant access code that you purchased online.

3. Click the link to *Keyboarding Pro DELUXE Online*. The program will present required components and ask you to install them. Depending on what is already installed on your computer, you may not have to install them all. On subsequent log ins, *KPDO* will go directly to the program.

Step 3: Enter the Course Code to Join the Class.

Locate the course code provided by your instructor. Double-click it with your mouse. Enter Ctrl + C to copy it; toggle (Alt + Tab) to the screen below and paste (Ctrl + V) the course code.

Read *KPDO. . . Your Tool to Success* page xi for help with using the software.

Path to Workplace Success...Capstone Project

SOFT SKILLS INTERVIEW WITH FOLLOW-UP ACTIVITIES

This project can be completed by a team or by each student individually. The team approach is recommended.

1. Your instructor will determine whether this is a team (3–4 members) or an individual activity and will provide a timeline for you to complete the activities.
2. Obtain contact information for team members if appropriate.

Part I – 15-Minute Face-to-Face Interview (Required of Each Student)

1. Each student must select an individual who hires, supervises, or manages employees in a career area of interest. The person may be in a company in which you or a family member is employed, someone from your neighborhood, your church, or other group with which you are affiliated.
2. Contact the individual and request an appointment for a face-to-face 15-minute interview. Explain that you are studying the importance of developing "soft skills" as part of your career preparation. Describe one or two soft skills you explored in this activity.
3. Use the Word Processor to key the five questions in item 4 below leaving about 2" of space after each question to take brief notes on the answers.
4. Conduct the interview and take brief hand-written notes.
   a. What soft skills are your strengths that helped you most to get your job and progress in your career?
   b. What soft skills do the people you manage need most?
   c. When you are hiring, how do you determine if a candidate has the required soft skills?
   d. How do you help your employees improve their soft skills?
   e. What advice would you give me about developing good soft skills?

Part II – Edit and Share Notes (Required for Both Teams and Individuals)

1. Edit and key your notes using complete sentences.
2. Share your notes with each team member **or** if you are working individually, share your notes with your instructor.

Part III – Selection of Five Most Important Soft Skills

Part III contains two options for students to determine what they believe are the five most important soft skills for workplace success based on interview data and their joint views or their individual views plus research data.

Option 1 is to be completed by students who are working in teams to make the decision.

Option 2 is to be completed by students who are working individually to make the decision.

 **Warmup**

1. Open *KPDO*.
2. Click the Word Processor button in the upper-right corner.
3. Key the paragraph using wordwrap (do not tap ENTER at the end of lines). Repeat if desired.
4. Click the Close button ⊠ in the upper-right corner to close the Word Processor; do not save it.

Good keyboarding skills are essential for almost all careers today. The time spent learning to key quickly and accurately is time well spent. Use good posture and good techniques to get you started on the right track. Then work diligently to achieve your speed and accuracy goals. Good keyboarding skills will save you time in preparing assignments for all of your classes. Also your work will impress your instructors.

Timed Writing

1. Click the Timed Writings tab.
2. Choose Pretest.

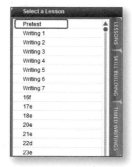

3. Choose 3' as the length; click Close.
4. Tap TAB to begin. Key from the textbook. Use wordwrap.
5. Repeat the timing for 3'.
6. Your results will be displayed in the Timed Writing Report.

Learning to key is just the first step toward developing a very meaningful career skill. The next step is to build both speed and accuracy. With basic keyboarding skills, you will be able to present information in an attractive format that is quite easy to read. You will also be able to develop your communication skills at the same time.

The next big step is to learn word processing. The software most often used in business organizations is Word, which is much more sophisticated than the basic word processor you used for your warmup. With Word you will be able to create attractive letters, memos, reports, and many other types of documents used in business.

One of the exciting things about working diligently to develop a skill is that you have the opportunity to set very specific goals and challenge yourself to meet them. Nothing is more motivating than being able to accomplish the goals that we set for ourselves. The incremental goals that you meet each day will result in major progress by the end of the course.

Path to Workplace Success...Develop Soft Skills

ACCOUNTABILITY

Accepting a position in the workplace indicates agreement and commitment to fulfilling the duties and responsibilities of the position and the expectations of the manager. The organization prospers when each team member consistently meets and exceeds the position's requirements and the expected goals. A few fundamental accountability practices are essential to be successful.

1. **Arrive on time.** Punctuality is an outward sign that the job is important to the employee, and arriving early to be ready to begin work at the starting time shows commitment to excellence.

2. **Stay on task.** With today's social media and cell phones, an employee is easily tempted to lose focus on tasks at hand to quickly check for messages or play a game. The expectation is for employees to complete work tasks on company time.

3. **Commit to quality work.** An excellent employee sets high standards beyond the minimum requirements and commits to excellence in all areas. Doing mediocre work is not an option.

4. **Hone organizational skills.** Prioritizing projects and meeting deadlines are critical to fulfilling job responsibilities. Acquiring organizational skills is essential.

5. **Devote time to professional development.** Growing in the job is also an outward sign of accountability. During performance review meetings, the employee and manager agree on areas of development that will assist the employee and the company.

For each of the scenarios below, you will complete an activity related to accountability. In the Word Processor, key a short explanation of what you have learned.

Scenario 1

Situation: You have a major report due in two weeks. Your team depends on your leadership and organizational skills to produce a quality product and to meet the deadline. You have a tendency to procrastinate.

Research: Locate at least four time management suggestions recommended by time management experts.

Apply: Select at least two strategies you will use to ensure this deadline is met with a quality product. What technology will you choose to assist you?

Write: Describe the two strategies you will use and identify the selected technology tool. Explain how these strategies will assist you in avoiding procrastination and meeting your deadline.

Scenario 2

Situation: Your manager is completing a task analysis for each employee to determine the needs of the organization. If you are a full-time student and not employed, keep the log for all your activities.

Research: Keep a log for one day (if you are a part-time employee, use the hours you work) and list all activities completed. Start at 8 a.m. and list every activity for each 30-minute increment until 5 p.m.

Apply: Analyze the log. Did you use time wisely? If not, how was time wasted? Could you rearrange work activities to achieve better results? Did you arrive on time? Did you begin work promptly?

Write: Describe at least two areas that you think were effective in your daily log. Explain at least two things you could have done differently that would have allowed you to be more productive.

Alphabetic Keys

LEARNING OUTCOMES

Lessons 1–10   *Alphabetic and Basic Punctuation Keys*

Lessons 11–13   *Review*

- Key the alphabetic keys by touch.
- Key using proper techniques.
- Key at a rate of 14 *gwam* or more.

Lesson 1   Home Row, Space Bar, Enter, I

Standard Plan   *For Using KPDO*

1. From the Lessons tab, select the lesson (Lesson 1).
2. Follow the directions on screen. Repeat the exercise for reinforcement or continue.
3. To end a lesson, view the Lesson Report.
4. Click the Log Out button in the upper-right corner.

    ✕ Log Out

5. Use these directions for all lessons.

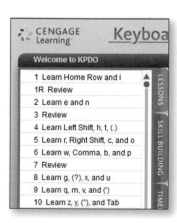

Path to Workplace Success...Develop Soft Skills

COMMUNICATION—MAKING A FIRST IMPRESSION

Building a strong network of professionals is essential on the path to success. Presenting yourself in a confident and energetic manner forms a positive first impression that opens the door to professional friendships. These five tips are highly recommended by communication experts.

1. **Initiate a conversation**. It's hard to build a network without starting a conversation, and often you are the one who must initiate the conversation. It's okay if you are shy—get over it.

2. **Give a firm handshake.** Show your interest and enthusiasm by giving a firm handshake—touching web to web. Please look at the person while shaking hands and do smile.

3. **Maintain direct eye contact.** Look at the person while talking and avoid the nervous tendency to look away. You do not want to give the impression you are nervous or bored.

4. **Present good posture.** Stand tall and do not slouch. Lean forward as you are talking to indicate interest in the other person.

5. **Dress appropriately.** Attention to one's dress conveys interest in the person you are meeting for the perhaps the first time. This first impression can determine the potential impact you may have on that person.

For each of the scenarios below, you will practice one of these essential communication skills. In the Word Processor, key a short explanation of what you learned in the practice activity.

Scenario 1

Situation: You have just been hired in an entry-level position, and you begin work in one week. You understand how important making a positive impression is—especially on the first day on the job. A proper handshake is the first skill you have decided to practice.

Think/Discuss/Research: What are the characteristics of a proper handshake for making a positive and powerful first impression? What are some poor techniques?

Apply: Pair with someone and practice shaking hands. For comparison, discuss and practice both effective and ineffective techniques.

Write: Describe the characteristics of a powerful handshake that you have learned are important for the first day on the job and every day.

Scenario 2

Situation: You are doing well in your position, but you know today will be important as you are sharing an idea at a team meeting. You know you must project confidence and have effective eye contact while in conversation with the team members.

Think/Discuss/Research: Why is eye contact important when sharing your ideas with your team or supervisor? What impression are you making?

Apply: With a group of at least three people, share an idea that you have. Topics might include (1) A suggestion you have for an improvement in your community or school; (2) How a person's dress has impacted your first impression of that person; (3) Time management strategies that have helped you in the past. Or, you can choose a topic with which you are comfortable. Your goal is to have eye contact with each person in the group by the conclusion of the conversation.

Write: Describe your experience. Did the topic make a difference in the quality of eye contact? Did you feel uncomfortable looking at your team while you talked? Did you receive any feedback from your team by looking at them? Did you feel nervous and feel the need to look away from your team? How can you improve your next conversation?

STANDARD PLAN   For Learning New Keyreaches

1. Find the new key on the illustrated keyboard. Then find it on your keyboard.

2. Watch your finger make the reach to the new key a few times. Keep other fingers curved in home position. For an upward reach, straighten the finger slightly; for a down reach, curve the finger a bit more.

3. Use these directions for learning all new keyreaches.

New Keys

1a Learn Home Row

Left Fingers   Right Fingers

HOME-ROW POSITION

1. Drop your hands to your side. Allow your fingers to curve naturally. Maintain this curve as you key.

2. Lightly place your left fingers over the **a s d f** and the right fingers over the **j k l ;**. You will feel a raised element on the **f** and **j** keys, which will help you keep your fingers on the home-row position. You are now in home-row position.

Note the curve of your fingers when your arms are hanging loosely at your side. Maintain this same curve when you place your hands on the home row.

Path to Workplace Success...Develop Soft Skills

CRITICAL THINKING AND DECISION MAKING

The ability to think critically helps you to make wise decisions that impact your work and your everyday life. Follow these five basic steps to make effective decisions.

1. **Identify the decision and collect facts**. Analyze objectively the situation requiring the decision. Get all the facts. Avoid making assumptions colored by stereotypes and preconceptions.

2. **Determine the options available**. Be creative in generating as many options as possible. In some cases options are predetermined.

3. **Analyze options carefully**. Try to view the situation from the perspective of everybody involved and from the organization. Examine consequences for each person and for the organization.

4. **Select the best option and implement it**. Evaluate all of the options and get more facts if needed. Also consider what is necessary for the option to be successful. The way a decision is implemented often determines its success.

5. **Evaluate the effectiveness of the decision implemented**. Did it produce the desired results? Can it be improved?

For each of the scenarios below, use the Word Processor to key the following information:

1. List the decision that must be made and the key facts to be considered. Add other things you think should be considered.

2. List the options available and the pros and cons of each.

3. Select the option and explain why it is best.

Scenario 1

Situation: Assume you live at home free and have saved enough money that you could (1) buy a small car so that you will have your own transportation, (2) you could use it to pay your tuition and other costs and avoid having to take out another substantial student loan, or (3) you could live in an apartment next year.

Facts: Family members lend you a car frequently when you need it. Most days you ride to classes with family or friends, but would prefer to have your own car. Public transportation to your college is available and inexpensive. Your family provides free living and tries to help you, but they are not in a position to pay your tuition. You already have heavy student debt that you will have to begin paying as soon as you complete your program.

Decision: What decision is in your best interest? Why?

Scenario 2

Situation: You have been looking for a part-time job, and you have two opportunities: One is for the Foundation that raises money for and supports your college. The other is a night job (6:00–11:00 p.m., 4 or 5 rotating nights a week) as the desk clerk at a local inn that is relatively inexpensive. With both jobs, you could work 20 to 30 hours per week. With the Foundation, you could work around your class schedule.

Facts: The Foundation duties include many that you are or will be studying—marketing, finance, accounting, management and office technology. You would be able to interact with donors and board members who generally are business executives. The Inn job duties include customer service skills, telephone skills, and basic office skills. The Inn job pays $1 more per hour than the Foundation job. Before you make your decision, search for information about desk clerk jobs in hotels and inns and about jobs in educational-type foundations.

Decision: Which job would be in your best interest? Why? What other information do you need to make a good decision?

SPACE BAR AND ENTER

Tap the Space Bar, located at the bottom of the keyboard, with a down-and-in motion of the right thumb to space between words.

Enter Reach with the fourth (little) finger of the right hand to ENTER. Tap it to return the insertion point to the left margin. This action creates a **hard return**. Use a hard return at the end of all drill lines. Quickly return to home position (over ;).

```
 1  j  jj  f  ff  k  kk  d  dd  l  ll  s  ss  ;  ;;  a  aa  jkl;  fdsa
 2  a  aa  ;  ;;  s  ss  l  ll  d  dd  k  kk  f  ff  j  jj  fdsa  jkl;
```

1c Practice Home Row

```
 3  ff   jj   ff   jj   fj   fj   fj   dd   kk   dd   kk   dk   dk   dk
 4  ss   ll   ss   ll   sl   sl   sl   aa   ;;   aa   ;;   a;   a;   a;
 5  fj   fj   dk   dk   sl   sl   a;   fjdk   sla;   fjkd   ls;a
 6  fff   jjj   fjf   fff   jjj   fjf   fjf   jfj   jfj   fjf
 7  ddd   kkk   dkd   ddd   kkk   dkd   dkd   kdk   kdk   dkd
 8  sss   lll   sls   sss   lll   sls   sls   lsl   lsl   sls
 9  aaa   ;;;   a;a   aaa   ;;;   a;a   a;a   ;a;   ;a;   a;a
10  f   j   d   k   s   l   a   ;   ;   a   l   s   k   d   j   f
11  ff   jj   dd   kk   ss   ll   aa   ;;   jj   ff   kk   dd   ll   ss   aa   ;;
12  fff   jjj   ddd   kkk   sss   lll   aaa   jjj   ;;;   fjdk   sla;
```

> **Keep your eyes on the textbook as you key each line.**

1d Textbook Keying

1. Key each line once. Tap ENTER at the end of each line.
2. Click Stop to end the exercise.

```
13  a  a;  al  ak  aj  s  s;  sl  sk  sj  d  d;  dl  dk  dj
14  j  ja  js  jd  jf  k  ka  ks  kd  kf  l  la  ls  ld  lf
15  a;   sl  a;sl  dkfj  a;sl  dkfj  a;sl  dkfj  asdf  jk
16  a;   sl  a;sl  dk  fj  dkfj  a;sl  dkfj  fjdk  a;a
17  f  ff  j  jj  d  dd  k  kk  s  ss  l  ll  a  aa  ;  ;;  fj
18  afj;  a  s  d  f  j  k  l  ;  asdf  jkl;  fdsa  jkl;
```

Path to Workplace Success...Develop Critical Skills

SKILLS REQUIRED FOR CAREER SUCCESS

The earlier you start planning and preparing for your career the more likely you are to be successful.

The skills required for specific jobs vary significantly depending on your field of interest, the organization that hires you, the type of job, and the level of the job. Regardless of these factors, a common base of knowledge and a common set of skills are required for virtually every job. These skills can be grouped into three categories:

- Technical skills
- Soft skills
- Conceptual skills

Technical Skills

Technical skills are especially important for entry-level positions. You will develop technical skills in the courses you take.

These skills include:

- Knowledge
- Expertise
- Ability to do the job

Examples of universal technical skills would be keyboarding skill, ability to use applications, such as *Word*, *Excel*, *Outlook*, and *PowerPoint*. The specific knowledge varies depending on the field, such as—manager, medical professional, or architect.

Soft Skills

Softs skills are critical at every level. The remainder of this section focuses on soft skills.

Soft skills are personal attributes, interpersonal skills, and emotional intelligence. Soft skills relate to the way you interact with other employees. Examples of soft skills that are required in most jobs include:

- Communication skills
- Creativity
- Critical thinking and decision making
- Ethics, honesty, and integrity

- Accountability and responsibility
- Teamwork and collaboration
- Time management and productivity
- Work ethic

Conceptual Skills

You will learn conceptual skills in advanced courses and on the job. Conceptual skills are required for advancement in your position.

Conceptual skills are the ability to see the big picture and how things fit together. Conceptual skills enable you to understand how your job fits into the overall business strategy of your organization.

1e i

© Cengage Learning

1f Improve Keystroking

1g Build Skill

1h End the Lesson
1. View Lesson Report.
2. Log out of the software.

19 i ik ik ik is is id id if if ill i ail did kid lid
20 i ik aid ail did kid lid lids kids ill aid did ilk
21 id aid aids laid said ids lid skids kiss disk dial

> *Use good posture; back and body erect; feet flat on the floor.*

22 as as ask ask ad ad lad lad all all fall fall asks
23 as asks did disk ail fail sail ails jail sill silk
24 ask dad; dads said; is disk; kiss a lad; salad lid
25 fill a sail; aid a lad; is silk; if a dial; a jail
26 is a disk; dads said; did fall ill; if a lass did;

i

27 id aid ail fail sail jail ails slid dill sill fill
28 aid lads; if a kid is; a salad lid; kiss a sad dad
29 as ad all ask jak lad fad said ill kill fall disks
30 is all sad lass a lid; is silk; silk disk; dad is;

AVAVA/Shutterstock.com

! WORKPLACE SUCCESS

Keyboarding: The Survival Skill

Keyboarding is a valuable and necessary skill for everyone in this technological world. It is an expected tool for effective communication throughout one's life.

Students who resort to "hunting and pecking" to key their school assignments are constantly searching for the correct letter on the keyboard. Frustration abounds for students who wish to key their research reports into the computer, but do not have the touch keyboarding skills required to accomplish the task quickly and proficiently. Students who can key by touch are much more relaxed because they can keep their eyes on the screen and concentrate on text editing and composing.

Web-Based Computing 3 Social Media

SOCIAL MEDIA

Most people think of the first generation of the Internet as a vast online collection of information that can be accessed easily and at little or no cost. The role of the Internet user is simply to access information in a passive way for whatever purpose the user needs the information. As the Internet has matured, most people now think of it as an interactive tool that enables the user to contribute and collaborate with others. The role of the user is that of participant in an activity generally thought of as social networking.

SOCIAL MEDIA TOOLS

Many options exist that enable users to participate actively. The group of social media tools listed below is one way of looking at just a few of the different options available to users who want to participate actively.

Social networks are generally thought of as tools for sharing information with an online community of people with common interests. Facebook, LinkedIn, and Pinterest are examples of frequently used social networks.

Micro-blogging sites enable users to send brief messages (often 140 or fewer characters) to a group of people which in turn can be sent to other groups. Twitter and Tumblr are examples of micro-blogging sites.

Video sharing sites provide a platform for people to post videos to share with others. YouTube, Metacafe, Break, and Google Video are examples of video-sharing sites.

Photo sharing sites provide a platform for people to post photographs to share with others. Examples include Flickr, Photobucket, Webshots, and Fotki.

Blogs are sites that provide publishing tools for people to post articles and various types of information to share with others and accept comments from readers. Examples of blog hosting sites include Blogger from Google, WordPress, and Live Journal.

Bookmarking sites allow users to bookmark or tag sites that they recommend. Examples are Delicious, Furl, Reddit, and StumbleUpon.

DRILL 3

SOCIAL MEDIA

1. Search for one article in each of the categories using the name of the category shown in bold as the keywords. Use the article as the basis for deciding which site in that category you will visit.

2. In each category, visit the website of one of the examples of sites listed.

3. Select one site in any of the categories and contribute something to the site. Post a photo, video, a blog, or whatever you would like to post.

Lesson 1R Review

Fingers curved and upright

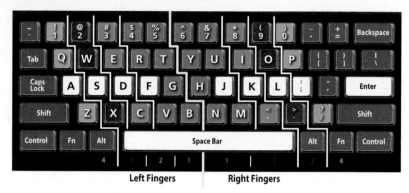

Left Fingers   Right Fingers

```
1 ff dd ss aa ff dd ss aa jj kk ll ;; fj dk sl a; a;
2 fj dk sla; fjdk sla; a;sl dkfj fjdk sla; fjdk sla;
3 aa ss dd ff jj kk ll ;; aa ss dd ff jj kk ll ;; a;
4 if a; as is; kids did; ask a sad lad; if a lass is
```

Skill Building

1Rb   Textbook Keying

1. Key each line once.
2. Click Stop to end the exercise.

Move fingers without moving your hands; eyes on textbook.

```
5 f  j  fjf  jj  fj  fj  jf  dd  kk  dd  kk  dk  dk  dk
6 s  ;  s;s  ;;  s;  s;  s;  aa  ;;  aa  ;;  a;  a;  a;
7 fj  dk  sl  a;  fjdk  sla;  jfkd  lsa;  ;a  ;a  ;s
8 f  j  fjf  d  k  dkd  s  l  sls  a  ;  fj  dk  sl  a;a
9 a;  al  aka  j  s  s;  sl  sk  sj  d  d;  dl  dk  djd
10 ja  js  jd  jf  k  ka  ks  kd  kf  l  la  ls  ld  lfl
```

1Rc   Improve Keystroking

```
11 f fa fad s sa sad f fa fall fall l la lad s sa sad
12 a as ask a ad add j ja jak f fa fall; ask; add jak
13 ik ki ki ik is if id il ij ia ij ik is if ji id ia
14 is il ill sill dill fill sid lid ail lid slid jail
15 if is il kid kids ill kid if kids; if a kid is ill
```

Build Skill and Game

When you finish the lesson, log out of *KPDO*.

Use the game to showcase your skills.

4. Select Upload.

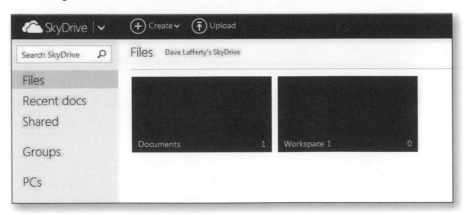

5. To add a file, click Upload and then select a document from your computer.

6. Select the desired file and it uploads. Double-click the file name to open and view it.

TIP

Some formats are not available for documents created on the SkyDrive.

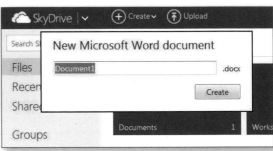

TIP

Many of the format commands are the same as the ones you used on the *KPDO* Word Processor.

7. To create a document, click Create and select *Word* document (see illustration above). The Word ribbon and screen displays. Key the document name in the Name box and click Save. Then key and format the desired document.

8. Click File and select Save when you have finished; close and exit SkyDrive.

DRILL 2

WEB APPS

1. Create a new document. Key the document and format it as shown in the illustration at the right.

2. Save the document as *My First SkyDrive Doc*.

Working on SkyDrive

The *Word* home tab ribbon is very similar to the Menu bar and the toolbar in the Word Processor in KPDO software. Creating a document on the SkyDrive is very easy and can be done without having *Word* software on the computer. An Internet connection and a browser are all that is necessary to connect to the SkyDrive and create or view documents.

Lesson 2 E and N

```
1 ff  dd  ss  aa  ff  dd  ss  aa  jj  kk  ll  ;;  fj  dk  sl  a;  a;
2 fj  dk  sl  a;  fjdk  sla;  a;sl  dkfj  dk  sl  a;  fjdk  sla;
3 aa  ss  dd  ff  jj  kk  ll  ;;  aa  ss  dd  ff  jj  kk  ll  ;;  a;
4 if  a;  as  is;  kids  did;  ask  a  sad  lad;  if  a  lass  is
```

New Keys

2b   E and N

e Reach *up* with *left second* finger.

n Reach *down* with *right first* finger.

e

```
5 e  ed  ed  led  led  lea  lea  ale  ale  elf  elf  eke  eke  ed
6 e  el  el  eel  els  elk  elk  lea  leak  ale  kale  led  jell
7 e  ale  kale  lea  leak  fee  feel  lea  lead  elf  self  eke
```

n

```
8 n  nj  nj  an  an  and  and  fan  fan  and  kin  din  fin  land
9 n  an  fan  in  fin  and  land  sand  din  fans  sank  an  sin
10 n  in  ink  sink  inn  kin  skin  an  and  land  in  din  dink
```

2c   All Reaches Learned

```
11 den  end  fen  ken  dean  dens  ales  fend  fens  keen  knee
12 if  in  need;  feel  ill;  as  an  end;  a  lad  and  a  lass;
13 and  sand;  a  keen  idea;  as  a  sail  sank;  is  in  jail;
14 an  idea;  an  end;  a  lake;  a  nail;  a  jade;  a  dean  is
```

CLOUD COMPUTING

Cloud computing is an evolving concept and, as such, is very difficult to define. Cloud computing can be simplified by examining the following concepts involved in cloud computing:

- A cloud computing system consists of many high-powered computer resources, such as servers, networks, storage applications, software applications, and information technology (IT) services that can be easily accessed with a basic computer and an Internet connection.

- The resources can be accessed anytime, from any location, and without any involvement of the organization providing the services. An example would be outlook.com or Gmail from Google. They are Web-based, available on demand, and accomplished without interaction with the provider.

- The IT services provided to businesses are fee-based services. Some services may be provided free, such as *Google Docs* and *Microsoft Web Apps. Microsoft Office 365* is now offered on a subscription basis with special fees for education use.

WEB-BASED EMAIL

If you have a Gmail or an Outlook.com email address, you are currently using cloud computing. You may previously have had a Hotmail account. *Microsoft* has replaced it with free email from Outlook.com. You will need an Outlook.com email account to work with Web Apps in the next section. If you do not have one, use your browser to go to Outlook.com. Note the option to *Sign Up Now*. Click it and follow the instructions to establish your account.

WEB APPS

You keyed a document about Web Apps in Drill 8, page 90 of the Word Processing section to help you learn about Web Apps. In this section, you will work with *Microsoft Web Apps* and learn how to view and to create a document on the SkyDrive. Your email address and your password serve as your ID.

To access the SkyDrive and add or create a document:
www.outlook.com

1. Sign in using your Outlook address and Password.
2. Hover the mouse over Outlook.
3. Click SkyDrive.

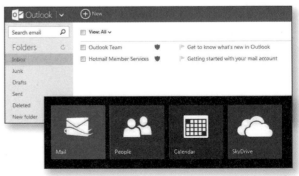

(continued)

Skill Building

2d Textbook Keying

1. Key each line once.
2. Keep your eyes on the textbook copy.

Reach with little finger; tap ENTER; return to home key.

15 if a lad;
16 is a sad fall
17 if a lass did ask
18 ask a lass; ask a lad
19 a;sldkfj a;sldkfj a;sldkfj
20 a; sl dk fj fj dk sl a; a;sldkfj
21 ik ik if if is is kid skid did lid aid laid said
22 ik kid ail die fie did lie ill ilk silk skill skid

i

2e Improve Keystroking

23 ik ik ik if is il ik id is if kid did lid aid ails
24 did lid aid; add a line; aid kids; ill kids; id is

n

25 nj nj nj an an and and end den ken in ink sin skin
26 jn din sand land nail sank and dank skin sans sink

e

27 el els elf elk lea lead fee feel sea seal ell jell
28 el eke ale jak lake elf els jaks kale eke els lake

2f Build Skill

29 dine in an inn; fake jade; lend fans; as sand sank
30 in nine inns; if an end; need an idea; seek a fee;
31 if a lad; a jail; is silk; is ill; a dais; did aid
32 adds a line; and safe; asks a lass; sail in a lake

Keep your eyes on copy; key words at a steady pace.

2g Textbook Keying

Key each line once.

33 send land skin faded sand kind line nine sale fail
34 dense sales lakes jaded likes jails salad kale inn
35 lad likes kale; lass likes silk; add a fee; is ill
36 kids in a lake; if in need; ask a lass; lad is ill

2h End the Lesson
Log out of *KPDO*.

Web-Based Computing:
Internet, Cloud, and Social Media

Web-Based Computing 1 Internet

OVERVIEW OF WEB-BASED COMPUTING

Three key components of web-based computing—Internet, Cloud, and Social Media—are covered in this section. These topics are overlapping and have many common advantages and disadvantages, but looking at them separately makes it easier to understand the concepts and to apply them in a useful manner.

INTERNET

Most students have had significant experience surfing the Web. If you haven't, a quick terminology review might be helpful.

Read the *Digital Citizenship* article on pages *REF10–REF11* to learn more about using the Internet effectively and safely.

Internet	A global collection of interconnected networks used to share information. To access the Internet, you must have an Internet connection and a browser.
Browser	A software program, such as *Internet Explorer*, *Chrome*, and *Firefox* that enables you to view web pages.
URL	A **U**niform **R**esource **L**ocater is a unique web address for each web page. Clicking the URL http://www.collegekeyboarding.com will take you to the College Keyboarding website. The protocol is **http://**, the location is **www** (World Wide Web), and the domain is **com** (commercial). Each segment of the address is separated by a period.
Search Engine	A software program, such as *Bing*, *Google*, and *Yahoo!* that enables you to locate specific information efficiently on the Web by using keywords that describe the topic.
Bookmark	A bookmark is a saved URL that you can access quickly by adding it to a **Favorites List**. To visit the website again, click Favorites and select it.

DRILL 1

WEB ACTIVITIES

1. Launch *Internet Explorer* or the browser on your computer.

2. Key the URL http://www.collegekeyboarding.com in the address box at the top of the page. Choose *College Keyboarding 19e*, and then choose *Keyboarding Course Lessons 1–25*. View the information available.

3. Click Favorites on the menu bar and select Add to Favorites. Click the Add button.

4. Click the Back arrow at the top of your browser twice to return to the opening page. Then key weather, your city, and state and click the Search Web button. Check your weather today.

Lesson 3 Review

home 1 ad ads lad fad dad as ask fa la lass jak jaks alas

n 2 an fan and land fan flan sans sand sank flank dank

i 3 is id ill dill if aid ail fail did kid ski lid ilk

all 4 ade alas nine else fife ken; jell ink jak inns if;

Skill Building

3b Textbook Keying

Key each line once.

Lines 5–8: Think and key words. Make the space part of the word.

Lines 9–12: Think and key phrases. Do not key the vertical rules separating the phrases.

easy words

5 if is as an ad el and did die eel fin fan elf lens

6 as ask and id kid and ade aid eel feel ilk skis an

7 ail fail aid did ken ale led an flan inn inns alas

8 eel eke nee kneel did kids kale sees lake elf fled

easy phrases

9 el el|id id|is is|eke eke|lee lee|ale ale|jill jak

10 is if|is a|is a|a disk|a disk|did ski|did ski|is a

11 sell a|sell a|sell a sled|fall fad|fall fad|fad is

12 sees a lake|sees a lake|as a deal|sell sled|a sale

3c Improve Keystroking

home row: fingers curved and upright

13 jak lad as lass dad sad lads fad fall la ask ad as

14 asks add jaks dads a lass ads flak adds sad as lad

upward reaches: straighten fingers slightly; return quickly to home position

15 fed die led ail kea lei did ale fife silk leak lie

16 sea lid deal sine desk lie ale like life idea jail

double letters: stroke double letters at a steady, unhurried pace

17 fee jell less add inn seek fall alee lass keel all

18 dill dell see fell eel less all add kiss seen sell

DRILL 22

COMPOSE FOLLOW-UP EMAIL

1. Compose an email that is a follow-up to the one you prepared in Drill 21. See specific instructions at the right.

2. Edit and proofread your email very carefully.

3. Close and click Next Activity to continue. (com-drill22)

Your instructor met with you and gave you many helpful suggestions about preparing for the interview. These suggestions included visiting the recreational center website and learning about the center prior to the interview, tips on dress and conduct during the interview, tips on the kinds of questions that are normally asked during interviews, and overall ways to present yourself more effectively. Your instructor agreed to serve as a reference for you.

Thank your instructor for taking the time to meet with you and indicate how much you appreciate the tips for interviewing that were provided. Be specific enough to show that you listened carefully and learned from the counseling session. Also thank your instructor for being willing to serve as a reference.

DRILL 23

COMPOSE PARAGRAPHS ABOUT CLOUD COMPUTING

1. Read information about the topic cloud computing from a variety of sources. Ideas for locating articles are listed below.

   a. *Web-Based Computing—Cloud Computing* section on pages 108–109.

   b. If you have access to the Internet, key the keyword phrase **cloud computing** and browse for pertinent information.

2. Summarize the information you read about cloud computing in your own words. Compose at least two paragraphs; double-space using the following as a suggested outline.

   a. Explain what cloud computing is and how it is used for communication.

   b. Describe some of the advantages of using cloud computing and some of the disadvantages.

3. Edit and proofread the paragraphs carefully.

4. Close and click Next Activity to continue. (com-drill23)

DRILL 24

COMPOSE PARAGRAPHS ABOUT SOCIAL MEDIA

1. Read information about social media and the variety of applications available to users today. Ideas for locating articles are listed below.

   a. *Web-Based Computing—Social Media* section on page 110.

   b. If you have access to the Internet, browse for pertinent information about social media tools. You may prefer to research one of the social media tools referenced in the article on page 110.

2. Summarize the information you read about social media applications in your own words. Compose at least two paragraphs; double-space using the following as a suggested outline.

   a. Explain what is and how social media tools are used for communication.

   b. Describe some of the advantages of using social media tools and some of the disadvantages.

3. Edit and proofread the paragraphs carefully.

4. Check; click Exit Word. (com-drill24)

5. Click Log out to exit *KPDO*.

3d Build Skill

```
19  and  and  land  land  el  el  elf  elf  self  self  ail  nail
20  as  as  ask  ask  ad  ad  lad  lad  id  id  lid  lid  kid  kids
```

phrases: think and key as phrases

```
21  if if|is is|jak jak|all all|did did|nan nan|elf elf
22  as a lad|  ask dad|  fed a jak|  as all ask|  sales fad

23  sell a lead|seal a deal|feel a leaf|if a jade sale
24  is a|is as if|a disk|aid all kids|did ski|is a silk
```

3e Textbook Keying

Key each line once.

© Cengage Learning

Tap Space Bar with down-and-in motion.

reach review

```
25  ea  sea  lea  seas  deal  leaf  leak  lead  leas  flea  keas
26  as  ask  lass  ease  as  asks  ask  ask  sass  as  alas  seas

27  sa  sad  sane  sake  sail  sale  sans  safe  sad  said  sand
28  le  sled  lead  flee  fled  ale  flea  lei  dale  kale  leaf

29  jn  jn  nj  nj  in  fan  fin  an;  din  ink  sin  and  inn  an;
30  de  den  end  fen  an  an  and  and  ken  knee  nee  dean  dee

31  el  eel  eld  elf  sell  self  el  dell  fell  elk  els  jell
32  in  fin  inn  inks  dine  sink  fine  fins  kind  line  lain

33  an  and  fan  dean  elan  flan  land  lane  lean  sand  sane
34  sell a lead; sell a jade; seal a deal; feel a leaf
```

3f Timed Writing

Key lines 31–34 for 1'.
If you finish before time
is up, repeat the lines.

Game

Log out when you
finish the lesson.

Showcase your keyboarding skills in the game.

DRILL 20

COMPOSE PARAGRAPHS

1. Write a paragraph of three to five sentences about each of the five topics.
2. Edit and proofread each paragraph carefully.
3. Close and click Next Activity to continue. (*com-drill20*)

1. Write a paragraph introducing yourself to your instructor. Describe the things you think are important in helping her or him get to know you better.

2. Write a paragraph describing one or more of your hobbies.

3. A relative gave you $500 today and suggested that you use it wisely. Write a paragraph discussing what you would do with the money and why you made that decision.

4. You have decided to become more physically fit. Therefore, you plan to improve your eating habits and become more physically active. Write a paragraph describing how you plan to achieve your goal.

5. Two summer jobs are available at a local recreational center. One job is for an assistant in the administrative office; the other is for an assistant to the recreation director.

   The job in the administrative office is varied and includes answering the telephone, scheduling appointments, working with visitors who come to the office, keeping basic records, and doing general office work.

   The job working with the recreation director is an outdoor job that involves coordinating activities for children in various sports, helping to teach children the sports and how to play together, and helping to maintain the various venues.

   Write a paragraph describing the job you would prefer and why you made that selection. Explain how you would be good for the job and how it would be good for you.

DRILL 21

COMPOSE AN EMAIL

1. Compose an email to your instructor following the instructions.
2. Edit and proofread your email very carefully.
3. Close and click Next Activity to continue. (*com-drill21*)

Describe the job that you selected in Drill 20 and why you chose it. Ask your instructor about the possibility of meeting with you at his or her convenience to help you prepare for your interview. Also ask if you may use her or his name as a reference.

Lesson 4 Left Shift, H, T, Period

Warmup *Lesson 4a Warmup*

home row 1 al as ads lad dad fad jak fall lass asks fads all;

e/i/n 2 ed ik jn in knee end nine line sine lien dies leis

all reaches 3 see a ski; add ink; fed a jak; is an inn; as a lad

easy 4 an dial id is an la lake did el ale fake is land a

New Keys

4b Left Shift and h

left shift Reach *down* with *left fourth* (little) finger; shift, tap, release.

h Reach to *left* with *right first* finger.

left shift

5 J Ja Ja Jan Jan Jane Jana Ken Kass Lee Len Nan Ned

6 and Ken and Lena and Jake and Lida and Nan and Ida

7 Inn is; Jill Ina is; Nels is; Jen is; Ken Lin is a

h

8 h hj hj he he she she hen aha ash had has hid shed

9 h hj ha hie his half hand hike dash head sash shad

10 aha hi hash heal hill hind lash hash hake dish ash

4c All Reaches Learned

11 Nels Kane and Jake Jenn; she asked Hi and Ina Linn

12 Lend Lana and Jed a dish; I fed Lane and Jess Kane

13 I see Jake Kish and Lash Hess; Isla and Helen hike

4d Textbook Keying

Key the drill once. Strive for good control.

14 he she held a lead; she sells jade; she has a sale

15 Ha Ja Ka La Ha Hal Ja Jake Ka Kahn La Ladd Ha Hall

16 Hal leads; Jeff led all fall; Hal has a safe lead

17 Hal Hall heads all sales; Jake Hess asks less fee;

Composition

Editing and proofreading usually make the difference between high-quality and mediocre writing.

Most careers require good writing skills. You can learn to be an effective writer with practice. Writing at the keyboard facilitates editing and is easier and more effective than handwriting documents. Editing requires complete focus on each of the following areas:

Content accuracy—Determine what needs to be included in a message and then check to see that necessary information is included and that all information is accurate.

Organization—Check sentence structure to see that ideas are presented logically and flow smoothly.

Writing style—Ensure that the message is clear, crisp, concise, and written at an appropriate level.

Mechanical correctness—Check for errors in grammar, spelling, punctuation, capitalization, number usage, and word usage.

COMPOSITION GUIDES

1. Begin with short, easy sentences and paragraphs on topics in which you have knowledge. Then work on putting the sentences and paragraphs together for complete messages.
2. Key your thoughts first and then edit them carefully. It is very difficult to write perfect copy when you begin keying.
3. Use familiar words and a simple, straightforward writing style.
4. Edit to ensure that sentences are carefully arranged, clear, and grammatically correct.
5. Structure paragraphs carefully, making sure that all sentences in the paragraphs relate to the same topic and that they flow logically.
6. Edit and proofread carefully.

DRILL 19

COMPOSE SENTENCES

1. Write and edit one to three complete sentences to answer the five questions.
2. Key the response to the question and tap ENTER twice between questions. Try to use an active, direct style of writing when possible.
3. Close and click Next Activity to continue. (com-drill19)

Example

Passive: I find baseball to be enjoyable, and I played well enough to be given the opportunity to play on the team.

Active: I enjoy playing baseball and earned a spot on the team.

1. Where do you live (street name, city or town, and state), and what do you like most and least about the place where you live?
2. Where do you attend school, and what do you like most and least about it?
3. What is your favorite subject, and why do you like it?
4. What is your least favorite subject, and why is it the least favorite?
5. How do you generally spend your time that is not spent in school or sleeping?

4e t and . (period)

t Reach *up* with *left first* finger.

. (period) Reach *down* with *right third* finger.

t

18	t tf tf aft aft left fit fat fete tiff tie the tin
19	tf at at aft lit hit tide tilt tint sits skit this
20	hat kit let lit ate sit flat tilt thin tale tan at

> **Space once after a period.**

. (period)

21	.l .l l.l fl. fl. L. L. Neal and J. N. List hiked.
22	Hand J. H. Kass a fan. Jeff did. Hank needs ideas.
23	Jane said she has a tan dish; Jed and Lee need it.

4f Improve Keystroking

24	I did tell J. K. that Lt. Lee had left. He is ill.
25	tie tan kit sit fit hit hat; the jet left at nine.
26	I see Lila and Ilene at tea. Jane Kane ate at ten.
27	tf .l hj ft ki de jh tf ik ed hj de ft ki l. tf ik
28	elf eel left is sis fit till dens ink has delt ink
29	he he heed heed she she shelf shelf shed shed she
30	it is if id did lit tide tide tile tile list list

Skill Building

4g Build Skill

31	he has; he had; he led; he sleds; she fell; he is
32	it is; he hit it; he is ill; she is still; she is
33	Hal and Nel; Jade dishes; Kale has half; Jed hides
34	Hi Ken; Helen and Jen hike; Jan has a jade; Ken is

4h End the Lesson
Log out of *KPDO*.

DRILL 17

PROOFREADING

1. Key the paragraph, correcting errors as you key. *Hint:* Ten errors are planted in the paragraph.

2. Follow the proofreading and editing procedures in the previous drill.

3. Check and click Next Activity to continue. (*com-drill17*)

The 1st quarter revenue figures for region IV was released today and you will be pleased to learn that once again the team exceded it's first quarter revenue budget. Congradulations! All member of the team exceeded their budget for the first quarter. We have consistently met both team goals for the passed 3 years; but rarely has every member of the team exceeded the budget plan.

DRILL 18

PROOFREADING

1. Key the document double-spaced, correcting errors as you key. *Hint:* Ten errors are planted in the two paragraphs.

2. Follow the proofreading and editing procedures in the previous drill.

3. Check and click Next Activity to continue. (*com-drill18*)

Email, once considered to be the most frequently used an misused means of communication is being surpassed by instant messaging and social networking applications, such as Facebook and Twitter. Blogs and wikis also accounts for many messages send in intoday's social networking society.

Taking advantage of these highly collaborative and targeted means of communication, businesses are creating their own social networking and micro-blogging sites. How ever, business executives share the following concerns: some lack of security for company information, the ease with which messages can be received by unintended recepients, communications being to causal, poor quality of messages, and inappropriateness of the medium for certain types of messages. To be a successful business communicator each employe must understand company communication policy and adhere to the established procedures and practices.

Lesson 4R Review

home row	1	sad lad hall lad sale ask jak add aka fall fad ha;
review	2	H. Le Ki J. tan tin hit at tat nat hat nit Lt. hid
all reaches	3	Jed is in sales; Kate ate fish. Hank hit his head.
easy	4	sit dial and land fit then half din hand lend disk

Skill Building

4Rb Textbook Keying

Key the drill once.

Think and key words and phrases.

words	5	slain tent Kent lent tea Jill Ned fed said laid he
phrases	6	he fakes | she hikes | his lead is safe | she and I fish
sentences	7	Nan is ill; Ed is at the lake; Jake is at the Inn.
sentences	8	Jed Hess did ski. Kit and I fished. Tina ate fish.
sentences	9	Hank ate his salad. Jane has the disk in the tent.
sentences	10	Ed said that Nate left the lake and is at the Inn.

4Rc Build Skill

11	shelf lead jiff lead sand find dine kind fend tent
12	kale sake takes deal tended salad jaded dined left
13	if I sell it; seek a deal; find a tent; at the Inn
14	He asked Ann; I need a fan; Ed sells jade and land.
15	Linda likes to hike; Dan likes to eat at the lake.

4Rd Timed Writing

1. Take two 1' timed writings. If you finish before time is up, begin again.
2. Use wordwrap.
3. When you are finished, log out.

X Log Out

Wordwrap: *Text within a paragraph moves automatically from one line to the next; tap ENTER only to begin a new paragraph.*

Use wordwrap ↓

```
               •        4         •         8        •
Janet sat in the tent, and then she fished at the
        12        •        16        •        20
lake. Eddie and his dad did find the disk in the tent
          •       24         •        28        •
at the lake. Helen and the dean ate a salad at the
        32        •        36        •        40
Inn. Then she asked the dean if he had a keen idea.
          •       44         •        48
She said the dean did have a keen idea.
```

DRILL 15

PROOFREADING

1. Key the paragraph, correcting errors as you key. *Hint:* Ten errors are planted in the paragraph.

2. Follow the proofreading and editing procedures in the previous drill.

3. Check and click Next Activity to continue. (*com-drill15*)

Blogs are Web logs (personnel journals) that is typically owned and maintained by 1 person. A blog gives it's owner a place to write about any topic of interest. It is typical updated frequently, much as a travelog or dairy would be. Only the owner can edit, delete, or add to the content of a blog. Visitors can comment about the content but they cannot change if. Wikis differ from blogs in this respect, since any body can change anything in a wiki.

DRILL 16

PROOFREADING

1. Proofread each sentence and then key the sentence correcting the error in it. Use the Numbering command to number each item.

2. Proofread again to ensure that you did not make any other keying errors. Correct any errors you find.

3. Check and click Next Activity to continue. (*com-drill16*)

1. The only way to proofread numbers effectively is too compare the keyed copy to the original source.

2. Concentration is an important proofreading skill, especially it you proofread on screen.

3. May people skip over the small words when they proofread; yet the small words often contain errors.

4. They sole 15 baskets at $30 each for a total of $450. Always check the math when you proofread.

5. Names are often spelled in different ways; there fore, you must verify the spelling to ensure that you use the correct version.

6. Reading copy on a word-bye-word basis is necessary to locate all errors.

7. Checking for words that my have been left out is also important.

8. Of course, you should also check to make sure the content in correct.

Lesson 5 R, Right Shift, C, O

Warmup *Lesson 5a Warmup*

home keys 1   a; ad add al all lad fad jak ask lass fall jak lad

t/h/i/n 2   the hit tin nit then this kith dint tine hint thin

left shift/. 3   I need ink. Li has an idea. Hank hit it. I see Kate.

all reaches 4   Jeff ate at ten; he left a salad dish in the sink.

New Keys

5b   r and Right Shift

r Reach *up* with *left first* finger.

right shift Reach *down* with *right fourth* finger; shift, tap, release.

r

5   r rf rf riff riff fir fir rid ire jar air sir lair

6   rf rid ark ran rat are hare art rant tire dirt jar

7   rare dirk ajar lark rain kirk share hart rail tart

left shift

8   D D Dan Dan Dale Ti Sal Ted Ann Ed Alf Ada Sid Fan

9   and Sid and Dina and Allen and Eli and Dean and Ed

10   Ed Dana; Dee Falk; Tina Finn; Sal Alan; Anna Deeds

5c   All Reaches Learned

11   Jane and Ann hiked in the sand; Asa set the tents.

12   a rake; a jar; a tree; a red fire; a fare; a rain;

13   Fred Derr and Rai Tira dined at the Tree Art Fair.

5d   Textbook Keying
Key each line once.

14   ir ir ire fir first air fair fire tire rid sir

15   fir jar tar fir flit rill till list stir dirt fire

16   Renee is ill. Fred read to her. Ed Finn left here.

17   All is still as Sarah and I fish here in the rain.

18   I still see a red ash tree that fell in the field.

19   Lana said she did sail her skiff in the dark lake.

DRILL 13

PROOFREADING

1. Key the paragraph, correcting errors as you key. *Hint:* Ten errors are planted in the paragraph.

2. Proofread the copy carefully on the screen. Make needed corrections. Preview the document and print it.

3. Proofread the hard copy carefully and mark any uncorrected errors, using proofreaders' marks.

4. Make the corrections in the document file.

5. Check and click Next Activity to continue. (*com-drill13*)

The executive committee plans to meet on April second at one o'clock in room 201 to develop a strategic plan to market our new products At it's last monthly meeting David Westfield, a leading Consultant with the Jones Group presented several alternatives. Mr Westfield will present a proposal at this meeting for consulting services from the Jones Group to assist us in planning the new product launch.

DRILL 14

PROOFREADING

1. Key the paragraph, correcting errors as you key. *Hint:* Ten errors are planted in the paragraph.

2. Follow the proofreading and editing procedures in the previous drill.

3. Check and click Next Activity to continue. (*com-drill14*)

Editing and proof-reading is just as important for internal documents as for external documents. However, many people wrong beleive that external documents need carefully scrutiny but documents that stay with in the company do not matter as much. If your e-mails are memos frequently contain errors, fellow workers and supervisors may think that you are careless or have poor communication skills. This perception may harm your chances for advancement within you company. Developing good communication skills, and applying those skills to each document that you produce will enhance your career opportunities.

5e c and o

c Reach *down* with *left second* finger.

o Reach *up* with *right third* finger.

c

20 c c cd cd cad cad can can tic ice sac cake cat sic
21 clad chic cite cheek clef sick lick kick dice rice
22 call acid hack jack lack lick cask crack clan cane

o

23 o ol ol old old of off odd ode or ore oar soar one
24 ol sol sold told dole do doe lo doll sol solo odor
25 onto door toil lotto soak fort hods foal roan load

Skill Building

5f Improve Keystroking

o/r
26 or or for for nor nor ore ore oar oar roe roe sore
27 a rose|her or|he or|he rode|or for|a door|her doll

e/n
28 en en end end ne ne need need ken ken kneel kneels
29 lend the|lend the|at the end|at the end|need their

c/o
30 ch ch check check ck ck hack lack jack co co cones
31 the cot|the cot|a dock|a dock|a jack|a jack|a cone

32 Carlo Rand can call Rocco; Cole can call Doc Cost.
all reaches 33 Trina can ask Dina if Nick Corl has left; Joe did.
34 Case sent Carole a nice skirt; it fits Lorna Rich.

5g Build Skill

i/t
35 is is tis tis it it fit fit tie tie this this lits
36 it is|it is|it is this|it is this|it sits|tie fits

37 Jack and Rona did frost nine of the cakes at last.
all reaches 38 Jo can ice her drink if Tess can find her a flask.
39 Ask Jean to call Fisk at noon; he needs her notes.

Proofreaders' Marks

#	Add horizontal space
‖	Align
~~	Bold
Cap or ≡	Capitalize
⌒	Close up
ℓ	Delete
∧	Insert
ˇ ˇ	Insert quotation marks
. . . or *stet*	Let it stand; ignore correction

/ or *lc*	Lowercase
⊏	Move left
⊐	Move right
⊓	Move up
⊔	Move down
¶	Paragraph
sp (circle)	Spell out
⌣ or *tr*	Transpose
___	Underline or italic

DRILL 12

PROOFREADERS' MARKS

1. Key the paragraph, correcting errors as you key. Refer to the proofreaders' mark at the top of the page.

2. Proofread the copy carefully on the screen following the guides above. Make appropriate corrections including your keying errors.

3. Preview the document and print it.

4. Proofread the hard copy carefully and mark any uncorrected errors using proofreaders' marks. Make the corrections in the document file.

5. Check and click Next Activity to continue. (*com-drill12*)

Instant messaging began as a popular tool for determining if friends were on line and were willing to play games or chat. Now its moving to the corporate setting. The number of instant messages send at work increased 110% last year. with IM, messages fly back and forth, faster then e-mail. Workers use IM to get urgently needed information, send important news signal that a client is waiting, and avoid telephone tag. 2 problems with instant messaging have been lack of security an the inability to keep a record of Correspondence. New business versions of Im software are addressing these issues.

Lesson 5R Review

r/c/o/right shift 1	circle order record Frank Sarah Tonia Henri candor
r/c/o 2	effort trick scroll control clone donor salon corn
right shift 3	Sandra Forde Addie Crone Stan Jackson Rhonda Caine
all reaches 4	Jeff drank his cold tea and ate cookies in a tent.

Skill Building

5Rb Textbook Keying

1. Key each line once.
2. Keep your eyes on the copy.

Think and key words and phrases as units.

words	5 choice rejoice north crank drank cross craft order
	6 creaked kitchen store lost frost train rained horn
phrases	7 to go north|I left at noon|reach up|he trusted her
	8 Fred chose one|Connie cooked|Daniel ate fried food
sentences	9 Carl and Jack left for a short train ride at noon.
	10 Lee and Jo can cook for their friends in the tent.

5Rc Build Skill

o/r	11 or cork for nor sore tore rote lore snore ore core
	12 his or her|she rode|at the door|she tore her skirt
c/o	13 close choose color cork corn coal ocean cold scorn
	14 close the door|choose a color|for a dock|cook corn
all reaches	15 Joan and Clark selected a nice color for the dock.
	16 Dick sent Lori a nice skirt and Frank a red shirt.

5Rd Timed Writing

1. Key a 1' timing; use wordwrap—do not return at the end of the line. If you finish before time is up, begin again.
2. Key a 1' timed writing at a slower but fluent pace.

wordwrap ↓

Connie said that her son can cook for her friends at noon. He is a trained chef and likes to cook for others. He can locate and choose the food. Harold offered to do all of the dishes. I think that is also a nice offer.

Proofreading

TIP

Learn to proofread on the screen first and then as a last check, proofread the printed document again.

Often the difference between high-quality and mediocre documents is in how carefully they are proofread. Careful proofreading ensures the accuracy of the final document.

Proofreading requires complete focus on each of the following areas:

Overall appearance of a document—check for appropriate stationery, attractive placement, and correct and consistent format.

Content accuracy—check for accuracy and completeness, such as making sure dates are correct and times are not left off.

Mechanical correctness—check for keying errors, as well as mistakes in spelling, grammar, punctuation, capitalization, word usage, and number usage. Review basic guides if you are not comfortable with your knowledge level in each of the areas listed.

PROOFREADING GUIDES

1. Check the document using the Spelling and Grammar commands.
2. Proofread the document on the screen slowly, on a word-by-word basis. Focus on words that may be spelled correctly but are misused, such as *you/your, is/in, if/it, there/their, two/to/too, then/than,* and *principle/principal.*
3. Check specifically for capitalization, punctuation, and number usage.
4. Check to see that the document is complete, ensuring that enclosure or copy notations are not left off.
5. Verify that each number is correct. The only way to ensure that a number is correct is to check it against the source from which it was keyed.
6. Preview the document on screen to ensure that placement is appropriate.
7. Print the document and proofread it again. It is helpful to use a guide (ruler, large envelope, or folded sheet of paper). Move it down line by line as you read. Mark the corrections using proofreaders' marks. Refer to a list of common proofreaders' marks found on the next page.

TIP

An error in a number could have significant negative consequences; for example, keying $300,000 rather than $400,000 in quoting a price or authorizing a loan at 7% when the correct percentage is 8% could prove to be very costly.

PROOFREADING STATISTICAL COPY

Statistical copy requires special attention. It is very easy to make errors in keying numbers, and it is very difficult to determine if a number keyed is correct. The same thing is true for a date or time.

1. Verify numbers against the original source; verify dates against the calendar; and check computations with a calculator.
2. Read numbers in groups. For example, the telephone number 618.555.0123 can be read in three parts: *six-one-eight, five-five-five, zero-one-two-three.*
3. Read numbers aloud and preferably with a partner checking against the original copy.

Lesson 6 W, Comma, B, P

KPDO **Warmup** *Lesson 6a Warmup*

home row	1	ask a lad; a fall fad; had a salad; ask a sad jak;
o/t	2	to do it; to toil; as a tot; do a lot; he told her
c/r	3	cots are; has rocks; roll cot; is rich; has an arc
all reaches	4	Holt can see Dane at ten; Jill sees Frank at nine.

New Keys

6b w and , (comma)

w Reach *up* with *left third* finger.

, (comma) Reach *down* with *right second* finger.

w

5 w ws ws was was wan wit low win jaw wilt wink wolf
6 sw sw w sow ow now now row row own own wow wow owe
7 to sew; to own; was rich; was in; is how; will now

, (comma)

8 k, k, k, irk, ilk, ask, oak, ark, lark, jak, rock,
9 skis, a dock, a fork, a lock, a fee, a tie, a fan,
10 Joe, Ed, and I saw Nan, Ann, and Wes in a new car.

6c All Reaches Learned

11 Win, Lew, Drew, and Walt will walk to West Willow.
12 Ask Ho, Al, and Jared to read the code; it is new.
13 The window, we think, was closed; we felt no wind.

6d Textbook Keying
Key each line once.

Good posture builds an attitude of preciseness.

14 walk wide sown wild town went jowl wait white down
15 a dock, a kit, a wick, a lock, a row, a cow, a fee
16 Joe lost to Ron; Fiji lost to Cara; Don lost to Al
17 Kane will win; Nan will win; Rio will win; Di wins
18 Walter is in Reno; Tia is in Tahoe; then to Hawaii

Spelling

References/Communication Skills/Spelling

DRILL 10

SPELLING

1. Proofread the sentences. If the word shown in bold is spelled correctly, key **Yes**. If the work is misspelled, key **No**.

2. Check and click Next Activity to continue. (*com-drill10*)

1. The sign in the store window stated that **turkeyes** are in the meat department.
2. Only cash or **checkes** are accepted in the new ice cream shop.
3. The postal clerk checked the **weight** of the package.
4. Students with fewer than three absences **recieved** special recognition.
5. Two **keys** were issued to each residence hall student.
6. How can celebrity chefs measure **accurately** without using a measuring spoon?
7. The complimentary closing very **truley** yours is seldom used in business correspondence.
8. You will find a list of school **supplies** in a display at the front of the store.
9. Be sure you have **submited** your travel budget request by the first of the year.
10. My parents traveled to Vermont for the turning of the **leaves**.

DRILL 11

COMPREHENSIVE REVIEW

1. Key the paragraph, correcting errors as you key. The ten errors include capitalization, number expression, subject-verb agreement, pronoun case and agreement, commas, and spelling errors.

2. Check and click Next Activity to continue. (*com-drill11*)

Scheduled for Monday june 15 at one p.m. in room two this week's orientation training session focuses on netiquette. in preparation for this meeting each participant are asked to bring thier three pet peeves regarding misuse of email instant messaging and discussion forumes. prizes will be awarded to the first 5 individuals whom register.

6e b and p

b Reach *down* with *left first* finger.

p Reach *up* with *right fourth* (little) finger.

b

19 bf bf bf biff fib fib bib bib boa boa fib fibs rob
20 bf bf bf ban ban bon bon bow bow be be rib rib sob
21 a dob, a cob, a crib, a lab, a slab, a bid, a bath

p

22 p; p; pa pa; pal pal pan pan pad par pen pep paper
23 pa pa; lap lap; nap nap; hep ape spa asp leap clap
24 a park, a pan, a pal, a pad, apt to pop, a pair of

Skill Building

6f Improve Keystroking

all reaches learned

25 Barb and Bob wrapped a pepper in paper and ribbon.
26 Rip, Joann, and Dick were all closer to the flash.
27 Bo will be pleased to see Japan; he works in Oslo.

reach review

28 ki kid did aid lie hj has has had sw saw wits will
29 de dell led sled jn an en end ant hand k, end, kin

s/w

30 ws ws lows now we shown win cow wow wire jowl when
31 Wes saw an owl in the willow tree in the old lane.

b/p

32 bf bf fib rob bid ;p p; pal pen pot nap hop cap bp
33 Rob has both pans in a bin at the back of the pen.

6g Build Skill

34 to do|can do|to bow|ask her|to nap|to work|is born
35 for this|if she|is now|did all|to see|or not|or if

all reaches

36 Dick owns a dock at this lake; he paid Ken for it.
37 Jane also kept a pair of owls, a hen, and a snake.

38 Blair soaks a bit of the corn, as he did in Japan.
39 I blend the cocoa in the bowl when I work for Leo.

Subject-Verb Agreement

DRILL 8

SUBJECT-VERB AGREEMENT

1. Key the sentences, choosing the correct verb. Use the Numbering command to number each item.

2. Proofread, check, and click Next Activity to continue. (*com-drill8*)

1. Everything in the packages (is/are) securely wrapped.
2. None of the mountains (is/are) visible today.
3. Many of the drivers (is/are) following too closely.
4. Everyone (is/are) expected to attend the seminar.
5. All of the candidates (was/were) invited to the debate.
6. Nobody (want/wants) to be left behind.
7. Few of the animals (is/are) outside today.

DRILL 9

SUBJECT-VERB AGREEMENT

1. Key the sentences, choosing the correct verb and applying the correct commas and capitalization. Use the Numbering command to number each item.

2. Proofread, check, and click Next Activity to continue. (*com-drill9*)

1. both of the curies (was/were) nobel prize winners.
2. mr. and mrs. thomas funderburk, jr. (was/were) married on Saturday november 23 1936 and they established their first home in Seattle Washington.
3. my sister and her college roommates (plan/plans) to tour london paris and rome this summer.
4. Emma Greer our new information manager (suggest/suggests) the following salutation when using an attention line: ladies and gentlemen.
5. the body language expert (place/places) his hand on his cheek as he says "touch your hand to your chin."
6. the japanese child (enjoy/enjoys) the american food her hosts (serve/serves) her.
7. the final exam (cover/covers) chapters 1-5.
8. Each of the directors in the sales department (has/have) given (his or her, their) approval.
9. According to bylaw 5-21 all of the candidates (are/is) invited to the debate at boston college.

Lesson 7 Review

Warmup *Lesson 7a Warmup*

© Cengage Learning

all | 1 | We often can take the older jet to Paris and back.
home | 2 | a; sl dk fj a;sl dkfj ad as all ask fads adds asks
1st row | 3 | Ann Bascan and Cabal Naban nabbed a cab in Canada.
3rd row | 4 | Rip went to a water show with either Pippa or Pia.

7b Improve Keystroking

5 | ad la as in if it lo no of oh he or so ok pi be we
6 | an ace ads ale aha a fit oil a jak nor a bit a pew
7 | ice ades born is fake to jail than it and the cows
8 | Ask Jed. Dr. Hand left at ten; Dr. Crowe, at nine.

Skill Building

7c Textbook Keying

Key each line once.

Keep your eyes on the textbook copy as you key.

9 | ws ws was was wan wan wit wit pew paw nap pop bawl
10 | bf bf fb fb fob fob rib rib be be job job bat back
11 | p; p; asp asp pan pan ap ap ca cap pa nap pop prow
12 | Barb and Bret took an old black robe and the boot.
13 | Walt saw a wisp of white water renew ripe peppers.
14 | Pat picked a black pepper for the picnic at Parks.

7d Build Skill

15 | Jake held a bit of cocoa and an apricot for Diane.
16 | Dick and I fish for cod on the docks at Fish Lake.
17 | Kent still held the dish and the cork in his hand.
18 | Ask far as I know, he did not read all of the book.

Pronoun Agreement

DRILL 6

PRONOUN AGREEMENT

1. For each sentence, select the correct pronoun from the two choices shown in parentheses.

2. Key just the correct pronoun for each sentence. Use the Numbering command to number each item.

3. Check and click Next Activity to continue. (*com-drill6*)

1. Each student must have (his or her, their) own data disk.
2. Several students have (his or her, their) own computer.
3. All candidates must submit (his or her, their) resume.
4. Napoleon organized (his, their) armies.
5. The company presented (its, their) five-year plan.
6. Jane and Alfredo sent (his and her, their) contribution.
7. Neither Chris nor Joseph wants to do (his, their) share.
8. Someone was talking on (his or her, their) cell phone and not watching the road.
9. Everybody should find a technique for stress management that works well for (him or her, them).

Commas

DRILL 7

COMMAS

1. Key the sentences, correcting the commas. Use the Numbering command to number each item.

2. Proofread, check, and click Next Activity to continue. (*com-drill7*)

1. The legislators voted on Policy #2083 on May 23 2015 at 5 p.m.
2. To view Michelle's entire social networking site I need her permission.
3. The parents volunteered to bring coffee juice milk and pastries.
4. Several club members designed an attractive logo and the fundraising committee created an online store for selling merchandise displaying the logo.
5. Mr. Rankin explained "Upload your essay to the class blog by Monday at 9 a.m."
6. The independent film festival will be held in Baton Rouge Louisiana on May 11-15.
7. Chef Nate I appreciate your answering my questions about organic gardening on your blog.

7e Textbook Keying

Key each line once.

words 19	a an pan so sot la lap ah own do doe el elf to tot
phrases 20	if it|to do|it is|do so|for the|he works|if he bid
sentences 21	Jess ate all of the peas in the salad in the bowl.
words 22	bow bowl pin pint for fork forks hen hens jak jaks
phrases 23	is for|did it|is the|we did a|and so|to see|or not
sentences 24	I hid the ace in a jar as a joke; I do not see it.
words 25	chap chaps flak flake flakes prow prowl work works
phrases 26	as for the|as for the|and to the|to see it|and did
sentences 27	As far as I know, he did not read all of the book.

7f Timed Writing

1. Take two 1' timed writings. If you finish before time is up, begin again.
2. Use wordwrap; do not tap ENTER at the ends of the lines.
3. End the lesson.

Goal: 12 *gwam*

wordwrap↓

gwam 1'

It is hard to fake a confident spirit. We will do   10
better work if we approach and finish a job and   19
know that we will do the best work we can and then   29
not fret.   31

| 1 | 2 | 3 | 4 | 5 | 6 | 7 | 8 | 9 | 10 |

7g Word Processor Timer

📄 Word Processor

1. Review the Standard Plan for Using the Word Processor Timer.
2. Key the timed writing from the textbook in 7f following the directions in the textbook.

STANDARD PLAN   for Using the Word Processor Timer

You can check your speed in the Word Processor using the Timer.

1. In the Word Processor, click the Timer button on the status bar.
2. The Timer begins once you start to key and stops automatically.
3. To save the timing, click the File menu and Save As. Use your initals (*xx*), the exercise number, and number of the timing as the filename. Example: *xx-7f-t1* (your initials, exercise 7f, timing1).
4. Click the Timer button again to start a new timing.
5. Each new timing must be saved with its own name.

7h Word Processor

1. In the Word Processor, key each line once for fluency.
2. Set the Timer for 30". Take two 30" writings on each line. Do not save the timings.

Goal: Reach the end of the line before time is up.

28 Dan took her to the show.
29 Jan lent the bowl to the pros.
30 Hold the wrists low for this drill.
31 Jessie fit the black panel to the shelf.
32 Patrick cooked breakfast for Jill and her friends.

DRILL 4

COMPOSITION

1. DS the paragraph, inserting a proper noun in each blank and applying correct capitalization and number expression.

2. Proofread, check, and click Next Activity to continue. (*com-drill4*)

last _____, my friend _____ and I had a holiday, so we decided to make the most of our day and take a bicycle trip to _____. before leaving, we stopped at _____ to purchase some high-energy foods to sustain us on our trip. we packed our saddle bags and left about _____ o'clock, traveling _____ on _____ street. although we were not on a sight-seeing trip, we did pass _____ and _____. by _____ p.m., we returned home exhausted from our journey of _____ miles.

Pronoun Case

References/Communication Skills/Pronoun Case

DRILL 5

PRONOUN CASE

1. For each sentence, select the correct pronoun from the two choices shown in parentheses.

2. Key just the correct pronoun for each sentence. Use the Numbering command to number each item.

3. Check and click Next Activity to continue. (*com-drill5*)

1. Was it Jane and (her, she) who starred in the movie?
2. The players who were injured were Dominique and (I, me).
3. With (who, whom) will you serve as an intern?
4. Our instructor invited (they, them) to the meeting.
5. (Who, Whom) will referee the game tonight?
6. Pat and (me, I) will be the pet sitters for Andy.
7. The problem with the delivery was between Joe and (they, them).
8. Lea and (he, him) had the highest scores on the test.
9. They bought expensive gifts for JoAnn and (I, me).
10. It was (her, she) who answered the phone.

Lesson 8 G, Question Mark, X, U

Warmup *Lesson 8a Warmup*

all 1 Dick will see Job at nine if Rach sees Pat at one.

w/b 2 As the wind blew, Bob Webber saw the window break.

p/, 3 Pat, Pippa, or Cap has prepared the proper papers.

all 4 Bo, Jose, and Will fed Lin; Jack had not paid her.

New Keys

8b g and ? (question mark)

g Reach to *right* with *left first* finger.

? Left SHIFT; reach *down* with *right fourth* finger.

> **Question mark:** The question mark is followed by one space.

g

5 g g gf gaff gag grog fog frog drag cog dig fig gig

6 gf go gall flag gels slag gala gale glad glee gals

7 golf flog gorge glen high logs gore ogle page grow

? (question mark)

8 ? ?; ?; ? ? Who?   When? Where? Who is? Who was she?

9 Who is here? Was it she? Was it he? Did Pablos go?

10 Did Geena? Did he? What is that? Was Joe here too?

8c All Reaches Learned

11 Has Ginger lost her job? Were her June bills here?

12 Phil did not want the boats to get here this soon.

13 Loris Shin has been ill; Frank, a doctor, saw her.

8d Textbook Keying

1. Key each line once.
2. Keep your eyes on the textbook copy.

reach review

14 ws ws hj hj tf tf ol ol rf rf ed ed cd cd bf bf p;

15 wed bid has old hold rid heed heed car bed pot pot

g

16 gf gf gin gin rig ring go gone no nog sign got dog

17 to go|to go|go on|go in|go in|to go in|in the sign

?

18 ?; ?;? who? when? where? how? what? who? It is he?

19 Is she? Is he? Did I lose Paul? Is Gabe all right?

CAPITALIZATION

1. Key the paragraphs, correcting all errors in capitalization.

2. Proofread, check, and click Next Activity to continue. (*com-drill2*)

as you requested, this past week i visited the facilities of the magnolia conference center in isle of palms, south carolina. bob bremmerton, group manager, was my host for the visit.

magnolia offers many advantages for our johns and lovett Leadership training conference scheduled for june 25-27. The prices are reasonable; the facilities are excellent; the location is suitable. In addition to the beachfront location, tennis and golf packages are part of the group price.

Number Expression

References/Communication Skills/
Number Expression

DRILL 3

NUMBER EXPRESSION

1. Key each sentence, correcting the number expression errors. Use the Numbering command to number each item.

2. Proofread, check, and click Next Activity to continue. (*com-drill3*)

1. Address the letter to 1 Elm Street and postmark by April 15th.

2. The retirement reception will be held on the 1st of May in Room Twelve at 5 o'clock.

3. Program participants included fifteen supervisors, five managers, and two vice presidents.

4. 12 boxes arrived damaged and about 2/3 of the contents were crushed.

5. The manager reported that 85% of the project was complete with 9 days remaining until the March 15th due date.

6. The presiding officer called the meeting to order at two p.m. and requested that the 2 50-page reports be distributed.

7. Nearly 10 million people visited the virtual museum this year.

8. Jim lives at nine 21st Street and works on 6th Avenue.

9. The attorney quoted from Section two of the code.

10. The parents of the Twin Cities Futbol Club have raised about 50 percent of the money for the tournament.

New Keys

8e x and u

x Reach *down* with *left third* finger.

u Reach *up* with *right first* finger.

Concentrate on correct reaches.

x

20 x x xs xs ox ox lox sox fox box ex hex lax hex fax
21 sx six sax sox ax fix cox wax hex box pox sex text
22 flax next flex axel pixel exit oxen taxi axis next

u

23 u uj uj jug jut just dust dud due sue use due duel
24 uj us cud but bun out sun nut gun hut hue put fuel
25 dual laud dusk suds fuss full tuna tutus duds full

Skill Building

8f Improve Keystroking

Think and key phrases.

26 Paige Power liked the book; Josh can read it next.
27 Next we picked a bag for Jan; then she, Jan, left.
28 Is her June account due? Has Jo ruined her credit?
29 nut cue hut sun rug us six cut dug axe rag fox run
30 out of the sun|cut the action|a fox den|fun at six
31 That car is not junk; it can run in the next race.

wordwrap ↓

8g Timed Writing

1. Take two 1' timed writings. If you finish before time is up, begin again. (The dot above various words equals 2 *gwam*; each number is another 4 *gwam*.)

2. Use wordwrap; do not tap ENTER at the end of lines.

3. Log out of *KPDO*.

Goal: 14 *gwam*

```
        •         4         •         8         •
How a finished job will look often depends on how
        12        •        16         •        20
we feel about our work as we do it. Attitude has
        •        24         •        28         •
a definite effect on the end result of work we do.
Tap ENTER once
        •         4         •         8         •
When we are eager to begin a job, we relax and do
        12        •        16         •        20
better work than if we start the job with an idea
        •        24         •        28         •
that there is just nothing we can do to escape it.
```

A review and quick check of basic communication skills, including capitalization, number expression, pronouns, commas, subject-verb agreement, spelling, proofreading, and composition, are presented in this section using activities in the *KPDO* software and drills provided here. To gain maximum benefit from this condensed review, always complete the pretest, review of the rules, and the posttest in *KPDO* first before completing other drills. Follow the path below each communication skill to locate the appropriate *KPDO* activities.

Capitalization

References/Communication Skills/Capitalization

DRILL 1

CAPITALIZATION

1. Key the sentences, correcting all capitalization errors. Use the Numbering command to number each item.

2. Proofread again to ensure that you did not make any other keying errors. Correct any errors you find.

3. Check and click Next Activity to continue. (*com-drill1*)

1. according to one study, the largest ethnic minority group online is hispanics.

2. the american author mark twain said, "always do right; this will gratify some people and astonish the rest."

3. the grand canyon was formed by the colorado river cutting into the high-plateau region of northwestern arizona.

4. the president of russia is elected by popular vote.

5. the hubble space telescope is a cooperative project of the european space agency and the national aeronautics and space administration.

6. the train left north station at 6:45 this morning.

7. the trademark cyberprivacy prevention act would make it illegal for individuals to purchase domains solely for resale and profit.

8. consumers spent $7 billion online between november 1 and december 31, 2010, compared to $3.1 billion for the same period in 2009.

9. new students should attend an orientation session on wednesday, august 15, at 8 a.m. in room 252 of the perry building.

10. the summer book list includes *where the red fern grows* and *the mystery of the missing baseball.*

Lesson 8R Review

Warmup *Lesson 8Ra Warmup*

reach review 1 Jack is glad about the response to the fundraiser.

p 2 The local paper printed their public opinion poll.

b 3 Four babies babbled as big bears rode brown bikes.

easy 4 The newest prices were not given to her and to me.

Skill Building

8Rb Textbook Keying

1. Key each line once.
2. Keep your eyes on the copy.

Move fingers up and down without moving your hands.

home row 5 add hash shall slash salads flags alfalfa fall ask

6 A fresh salad dish was added for staff and guests.

third row 7 tire wrote rewrite ripe proper papers trip picture

8 A reporter edited the newspaper stories with ease.

1st/2nd fingers 9 returned guest changes kicked tonight flight drink

10 Ed kept doing kind deeds for the children in need.

8Rc Timed Writing

1. Take two 1' timed writings. If you finish before time is up, begin again.
2. Use wordwrap; do not tap ENTER at the ends of the lines.

gwam 1'

Luck comes to those who are prepared for it. Think 10
about what is needed to be where one should be in a 21
decade. What will it take? Will it take additional 31
education or perhaps just other experience? One sets 41
a large goal and then works through a series of other 52
lesser goals to get there. One needs to be able to 62
know what success looks like as one finishes one of 73
the goals to get to the next one. If one does it 83
well, people will think it was all luck. 91

| 1 | 2 | 3 | 4 | 5 | 6 | 7 | 8 | 9 | 10 |

8Rd Enrichment

Word Processor

1. In the Word Processor, key two 30" timings on each line. Try to increase your speed the second time.
2. Log out of *KPDO*.

We use the web and work online.

We shop online and use social networks.

The web helps us as we work and share data.

While working online, we need to keep our data safe.

PERSONAL BUSINESS LETTER

1. Key the letter at the right following the Personal Business Letter Guidelines.

2. Save as *wp-drill9*.

3. Design and prepare a personal business letterhead for yourself. Use colors, fonts, and borders of your choice.

4. Save as *wp-drill10*.

Mark A. and Lauren C. Johnson

47 Mahalo Lane * Columbia, SC 29204-3380 * 803.555.0166 * Fax 803.555.0184 * Johnson@hotmail.com

2" Current date ↓ 4

Mr. Joseph C. Holbrook
JH Safari Company
1240 N. Astor Street
Chicago, IL 60610-2308 ↓ 2

Dear Mr. Holbrook ↓ 2

Thank you for sending us the final itinerary and the preliminary documentation for our African safari. The revised itinerary is exactly what we expected, and we are especially pleased with the reservations made at both the camp on the Zambezi River in Zambia and the private game reserve in South Africa. ↓ 2

The preliminary documentation was very helpful. We have verified that our passports have more than six months prior to expiration and more than six blank pages. However, we have elected to wait and acquire the necessary visas at the borders of the countries requiring visas because it is easy to do and less expensive than using the service to acquire them prior to our departure. Our local physician has administered the required vaccinations, prescribed appropriate malaria prevention drugs, and provided us with signed copies of the International Certificate of Vaccination. ↓ 2

The enclosed travel form has been completed and signed. The medical and travel insurance information has been added to the form as requested. We look forward to receiving the final documentation and to having a wonderful experience on our first safari. ↓ 2

Sincerely ↓ 4

Lauren C. Johnson

Lauren C. Johnson ↓ 2

Enclosure

Lesson 9 Q, M, V, Apostrophe

Warmup *Lesson 9a Warmup*

all letters	1	Lex gripes about cold weather; Fred is not joking.
space bar	2	Is it Di, Jo, or Al? Ask Lt. Coe, Bill; She knows.
easy	3	We did rush a bushel of cut corn to the six ducks.
easy	4	He is to go to the Tudor Isle of England on a bus.

New Keys

9b q and m

q Reach *up* with *left fourth* finger.

m Reach *down* with *right first* finger.

q

5 q qa qa quad quad quaff quant queen quo quit quick

6 qa qu qa quo quit quod quid quip quads quote quiet

7 quite quilts quart quill quakes quail quack quaint

m

8 m mj mj jam man malt mar max maw me mew men hem me

9 m mj ma am make male mane melt meat mist amen lame

10 malt meld hemp mimic tomb foam rams mama mire mind

9c All Reaches Learned

11 Quin had some quiet qualms about taming a macaque.

12 Jake Coxe had questions about a new floor program.

13 Max was quick to join the big reception for Lidia.

9d Textbook Keying

1. Key each line once; keep your elbows at your side.
2. Keep your eyes on the textbook copy.

m/x
14 me men ma am jam am lax, mix jam; the hem, six men

15 Emma Max expressed an aim to make a mammoth model.

q/u
16 qa qu aqua aqua quit quit quip quite pro quo squad

17 Did Quin make a quick request to take the Qu exam?

g/n
18 fg gn gun gun dig dig nag snag snag sign grab grab

19 Georgia hung a sign in front of the union for Gib.

Personal business letters should adhere to the same general guidelines as business letters. Letters consist of three main parts: the opening lines to the receiver (date, letter address, and salutation), the body of the message, and the writer's closing lines (complimentary close, name, title, and enclosures if any). Standard letter parts are illustrated below.

Typically, personal business letters are prepared using block letter format with open punctuation. All letter parts are keyed at the left margin and punctuation is not used after the salutation or complimentary close.

Personal business letterhead can be easily designed using fonts, colors, and borders in the Open Screen of *KPDO*. The letterhead shown has a .75" top margin, blue Vladimir Script 24-point font for the name followed by a 1/4-point blue line, and then blue Arial 9-point font for the address line.

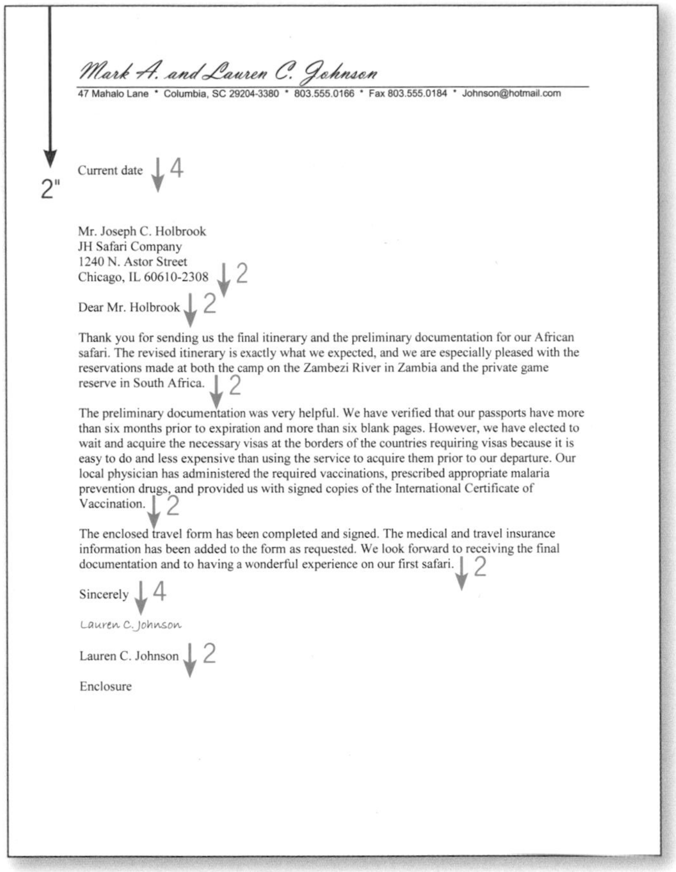

Dateline: Date letters as of date prepared and position at 2" or at least 0.5" below the letterhead.

Letter address: Include personal title, name, professional title (if known), company name, street address, city, state, and ZIP Code. Position four lines below date.

Salutation (or Greeting): Position two lines below the letter address and use a courtesy title (Mr., Ms., or Dr.). Use Ladies and Gentlemen when addressing a company. Do not use punctuation.

Body: Position two lines below the salutation.

Complimentary close: Position two lines below the body. Capitalize only the first letter. Do not use punctuation.

Signature: Writer should sign the letter or affix an electronic signature between the complimentary close and the writer's name.

Writer's name: Position four lines below the complimentary close. Include a personal title to indicate gender only when the writer's name is not gender specific, such as Pat or Lynn or initials are used, and when the recipient does not know the writer.

Enclosure: Position an enclosure notation two lines below the writer's name if material is enclosed.

Mark A. and Lauren C. Johnson
47 Mahalo Lane * Columbia, SC 29204-3380 * 803.555.0166 * Fax 803.555.0184 * Johnson@hotmail.com

2"

Current date ↓4

Mr. Joseph C. Holbrook
JH Safari Company
1240 N. Astor Street
Chicago, IL 60610-2308 ↓2

Dear Mr. Holbrook ↓2

Thank you for sending us the final itinerary and the preliminary documentation for our African safari. The revised itinerary is exactly what we expected, and we are especially pleased with the reservations made at both the camp on the Zambezi River in Zambia and the private game reserve in South Africa. ↓2

The preliminary documentation was very helpful. We have verified that our passports have more than six months prior to expiration and more than six blank pages. However, we have elected to wait and acquire the necessary visas at the borders of the countries requiring visas because it is easy to do and less expensive than using the service to acquire them prior to our departure. Our local physician has administered the required vaccinations, prescribed appropriate malaria prevention drugs, and provided us with signed copies of the International Certificate of Vaccination. ↓2

The enclosed travel form has been completed and signed. The medical and travel insurance information has been added to the form as requested. We look forward to receiving the final documentation and to having a wonderful experience on our first safari. ↓2

Sincerely ↓4

Lauren C. Johnson

Lauren C. Johnson ↓2

Enclosure

9e v and ' (apostrophe)

v Reach *down* with *left first* finger.

' Reach to the *right* with the *right fourth* finger.

Apostrophe: The apostrophe shows (1) omission (as Rob't for Robert or it's for it is) or (2) possession when used with nouns (as Joe's hat).

v

20 v vf vf vie vie via via vim vat vow vile vale vote
21 vf vf ave vet ova eve vie dive five live have lave
22 cove dove over aver vivas hive volt five java jive

' (apostrophe)

23 '; '; it's it's Rod's; it's Bo's hat; we'll do it.
24 We don't know if it's Lee's pen or Norma's pencil.
25 It's ten o'clock; I won't tell him that he's late.

Skill Building

9f Improve Keystroking

26 It's Viv's turn to drive Iva's van to Ava's house.
v/? 27 Qua, not Vi, took the jet; so did Owen. Didn't he?
28 Wasn't Vada Baxter a judge at the post garden show?
29 Viola said she has moved six times in five months.
30 Does Dave live on Vines Avenue? Must he leave now?
q/? 31 Did Viv vote? Can Paque move it? Did Valerie quit?
32 Didn't Raquel quit Carl Quent after their quarrel?

9g Timed Writing

1. Take a 1' timing on each paragraph. If you finish before time is up, start the paragraph again. The dots equal 2 words. Use wordwrap.

2. Finish the lesson; log out of *KPDO*.

wordwrap ↓

```
         •          4          •          8          •
The questions of time use are vital ones; we miss
          12          •          16          •          20
so much just because we don't plan. If we structure
          •          24          •          28
our week, we save time for those extra premium
  •          30          •
things we long to do.
          •          4          •          8          •
List the tasks to be done for the week and then
  •          12          •          16          •          20
place importance on each one. Complete the tasks in
          •          24
order of importance.
```

FORMATS, LINE SPACING, FONTS

1. Key the text without the character formats.
2. Save as *wp-drill7*.
3. Select the appropriate text and apply formats shown.
4. Select WEB APPS and apply 14-point font.
5. Save *wp-drill7* again and print. Do not close.
6. Select paragraphs 1 and 2 and apply Double Spacing.
7. Save as *wp-drill7r* and print.

WEB APPS

The Word Processor you are using to complete these activities is hosted by your computer. To use the Word Processor, you accessed it by clicking the *Word Processor* button in your **KPDO software**.

Similar Word Processors are hosted on the Internet. To access a Word Processor on the Internet, you use an <u>Internet connection</u> and a <u>Web browser</u>. These online Word Processors are generally called Web apps or Web applications.

FORMATS, CENTER PAGE

1. Key the text applying the formats shown.
2. Center the page:
   a. Click the Format tab and then click Page Settings from the list of options on the menu.
   b. On the Page Parameters dialog box, in the Vertical Alignment box, click the down arrow and choose Center. Click OK.
3. Save as *wp-drill8*; print.

Center ⟶ WEB APPS

Align Left ⟶ Web apps provide both the Word Processor and storage space on the Internet. Documents stored on the Internet can be viewed and edited. New documents can also be created.

Justify ⟶ Documents stored on the Web can be accessed on the Internet with a browser at any time and from any location. Word processing software is not necessary on the computer used to access the documents. The two best-known word processing Web apps are listed below.

Center ⟶ *Google Docs*
Microsoft Office Web Apps

Align Right ⟶ For more information, contact:
Your Name
803.555.0126

Lesson 9R Review

all reaches 1 Quij produces both fine work and excellent volume.

g/? 2 Did he go? Where is Gianna? Did George go golfing?

b/p 3 Paul has pictures of bears, bats, pigs, and bison.

easy 4 Paige is to go in a taxi to the address we stated.

Skill Building

Work for smoothness, not speed.

9Rb Textbook Keying

1. Key each line once.
2. Keep your eyes on the copy.

Apostrophe 5 I'll she'll o'clock we're didn't she's isn't don't

6 one's job; Donnel's, gov't, it's time; p's and q's

7 Spell out it's, doesn't, can't, gov't, and she'll.

q 8 netiquette queue quench quad FAQ quotes quit quest

9 Quen asked a question; eat a quince; make it quick

10 Quotes on quotas of useful equipment are required.

v 11 voice invert evoke vital prove event vacuum valid

12 improve best speed; strive high; have clear vision

13 Dev found five favorite websites for French class.

9Rc Timed Writing

1. Take two 1' timings on paragraph 1. If you finish before time is up, begin again.
2. Take a 2' timing on both paragraphs.
3 Log out of *KPDO* when you are finished.

Goal: 13 *gwam*

wordwrap   *gwam* 1' 2'

	1'	2'
Drill practice is a good thing to do to help with	10	5
speed and control. To get the most out of practice,	20	10
use the drills that help with the most common	30	15
problems. Finger and row drills are often used. Work	40	20
is often needed with the first, second, third, and	50	25
fourth fingers and rows. Work on the use of the shift	61	31
for capital letters as needed.	67	34
Work with double letters and letters next to each	10	39
other, as these letters often cause problems in	20	43
words. Spacing can also be a major concern, so	29	48
practice in the use of the space bar will help. Be	39	53
sure to review the required drills, and work on what	50	59
seems to help the most.	54	61

1' | 1 | 2 | 3 | 4 | 5 | 6 | 7 | 8 | 9 | 10 |
2' | 1 | 2 | 3 | 4 | 5 |

Character Formats

Sometimes you may want to emphasize or enhance the appearance of text. Attributes such as bold, underline, italic, fonts, and font sizes apply to characters. Use the Toolbar to access these formats. To be most efficient, key the text and then format it. To apply formats to text that has already been keyed, select the text and click the appropriate format button.

Paragraph Formats

Each time you tap ENTER, the Word Processor inserts a paragraph mark (¶) and starts a new paragraph. A paragraph may consist of a single line followed by a hard return (¶ mark) or several lines that wrap and are followed by a hard return. Paragraph formats include alignment, line spacing, and tabs. To view hard returns or paragraphs, choose **View** menu, **Show codes**.

Paragraph formats such as alignment, tabs, and line spacing apply to an entire paragraph. Paragraph formats can be applied to existing text by selecting the text and applying the format. To apply a paragraph format as you key, select the format and key the text. The feature will be "turned on" until you click the turn it off.

Alignment

The alignment commands are located on the toolbar and include: Align Left, Center, Align Right, and Justify. To align existing text, select the text and apply the format. Alignment is a paragraph command.

Line Spacing

The default line spacing is single; to change line spacing, position the insertion point in the paragraph you wish to change. Click the Format tab on the menu bar and select Paragraph; then click Double Space. To change multiple paragraphs, select the paragraphs first.

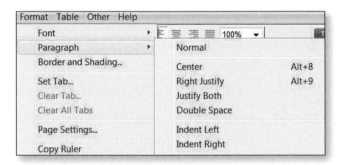

DRILL 6

FORMATS

1. Key each of the sentences, applying the format as you key. Save as *wp-drill6*. Print.

2. Clear the screen (click the New button).

1. **These words are keyed in bold.**

2. *These words are keyed in italic.*

3. <u>These words are underlined.</u>

4. This line is keyed in 14 point.

Lesson 10 Z, Y, Quotation Mark, Tab

Warmup *Lesson 10a Warmup*

all letters	1	Quill owed those back taxes after moving to Japan.
spacing	2	Didn't Vi, Max, and Quaid go? Someone did; I know.
q/v/m	3	Marv was quite quick to remove that mauve lacquer.
easy	4	Lana is a neighbor; she owns a lake and an island.

New Keys

10b Learn z and y

z Reach *down* with *left fourth* finger.

y Reach *up* with *right first* finger.

Curve the little finger tightly to reach down and in for the z key.

z

5 za za zap zap zing zig zag zoo zed zip zap zig zed

6 doze zeal zero haze jazz zone zinc zing size ozone

7 ooze maze doze zoom zarf zebus daze gaze faze adze

y

8 y yj yj jay jay hay hay lay nay say days eyes ayes

9 yj ye yet yen yes cry dry you rye sty your fry wry

10 ye yen bye yea coy yew dye yaw lye yap yak yon any

10c All Reaches Learned

11 Did you say Liz saw any yaks or zebus at your zoo?

12 Relax; Jake wouldn't acquire any favorable rights.

13 Has Zack departed? Alex, Joy, and I will go alone.

10d Textbook Keying
Key each line once.

14 Cecilia brings my jumbo umbrella to every concert.

direct reach 15 John and Kim recently brought us an old art piece.

16 I built a gray brick border around my herb garden.

17 sa ui hj gf mn vc ew uy re io as lk rt jk df op yu

Adjacent reach 18 In Ms. Lopez' opinion, the opera was really great.

19 Polly and I were joining Walker at the open house.

Insert/Delete

Insert and Delete features are used to correct errors or revise documents.

Insert: To insert text, simply position the insertion point at the location where the new text is to appear and key the text. Existing text moves to the right.

Delete: The DELETE key erases text that is no longer needed.

To delete a character: Position the insertion point to the left of the character to delete and tap DELETE or position the insertion point to the right of the character to delete and tap BACKSPACE. Be careful not to hold down the delete or backspace keys since they will continue to erase characters.

To delete a word: Double-click the word to be deleted and tap DELETE.

Select

Select identifies text that has been keyed so that it can be modified. Selected text appears black on the screen. Select text using the mouse.

To select text	Position the insertion point on the first character to be selected. Click the left mouse button and drag the mouse over the text to be selected. To deselect after each item click the mouse again.
To select a word	Double-click the word.
To select a paragraph	Triple-click in the paragraph.
To select multiple lines	Click the left mouse button and drag in the area left of the lines.

DRILL 5

EDIT TEXT

1. Make the deletions shown at the right. (Your document will be single-spaced.)
2. Correct any other errors you may have made.
3. Save as *wp-drill5*.
4. Click the Print button on the toolbar.
5. Use the mouse to select each of the following items. Deselect after each item.
   - The first sentence.
   - The word Serendipity in paragraph 1.
   - All of paragraph 1.
   - The entire document.
6. Move the insertion point to the beginning of the document. Key your name at the left margin. Tap ENTER four times. Do not save or print.

Serendipity, a ~~new homework~~ research tool from Information Technology Company, is available to subscribers of ~~the major~~ online services via the World Wide Web.

Offered as a subscription service aimed at ~~college~~ students, Serendipity is a collection of tens of thousands of articles from ~~major~~ encyclopedias, reference books, magazines, pamphlets, and Internet sources combined into a single searchable database.

Serendipity puts an electronic library right at students' fingertips with just a computer and an Internet connection. The program offers two browse-and-search capabilities. Users can find articles on just about any subject by entering questions in simple question format or browse the database by pointing and clicking on key words that identify related articles. For more information, call 1.800.555.0174 or address email to lab@serendipity.com.

New Keys

10e Learn " (quotation mark) and TAB

" Shift; then reach to the *right* with the *right fourth* finger.

TAB Reach *up* with *left fourth* finger.

" (quotation mark)

20 "; "; " " "web" "media" "videos" I like "texting."
21 "I am not," she said, "going." I just said, "Why?"

TAB key

22   The tab key is used for indenting paragraphs
and aligning columns.

23   Tabs that are set by the software are called
default tabs, which are usually a half inch.

Skill Building

10f Textbook Keying

Key each line once. Tap TAB to indent each paragraph. Use wordwrap, tapping ENTER only at the end of each paragraph.

24   The expression "I give you my word," or put another
25 way, "Take my word for it," is just a way I can say, "I
26 prize my name; it clearly stands in back of my words."
27 I offer "honor" as collateral.
tab 28   Tap the tab key and begin the line without a pause
to maintain fluency.

29   She said that this is the lot to be sent; I
agreed with her.

30   Tap Tab before starting to key a timed writing
so that the first line is indented.

10g Timed Writing

1. Take two 1' timed writings. If you finish before time is up, begin again.
2. End the lesson and log out of *KPDO*.

Goal: 15 *gwam*

E **ALL LETTERS**

wordwrap *gwam* 1'

Tab → All of us work for progress, but it is not   9
always easy to analyze "progress." We work hard for   19
it; but, in spite of some really good efforts, we may 29
fail to get just exactly the response we want.   39

Tab → When this happens, as it does to all of us, it   9
is time to cease whatever we are doing, have a quiet   20
talk with ourselves, and face up to the questions   29
about our limited progress. How can we do better?   39

| 1 | 2 | 3 | 4 | 5 | 6 | 7 | 8 | 9 | 10 |

Help

Use the Help button to answer questions you may have about the software.

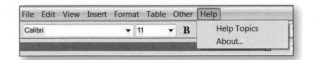

DRILL 1

FILE, EDIT, AND FORMAT TABS ON MENU BAR

1. Click the File tab on the Menu bar. Observe the items on the File menu.

2. Click Open to display the Open dialog box; click Cancel to close it.

3. Click the Edit tab on the Menu bar; view the items listed.

4. Click the Format tab to view the Format menu.

DRILL 2

HELP AND PRINT

1. Click the Help tab on the Menu bar, then Help Topics.

2. Select Navigating the software and click Navigating the *KPDO* Homepage.

3. Use the Scroll bar to view all of the information.

4. Click the Print command at the top of the Help dialog box to print the information.

DRILL 3

INSERT TAB ON MENU BAR

1. Click the Insert tab on the Menu bar, then select Symbol.

2. Select the Special Characters tab and view the options.

3. Click Done to close the Symbol dialog box.

DRILL 4

CREATE PARAGRAPH

1. Key the paragraph.

2. Click the Save button. Key **wp-drill4** in the File name box.

3. Click the New button. You now have a clear screen.

4. Click Open button. Click *drill-4* then OK to open Drill 4.

5. Position the insertion point at the beginning of Sentence 2. Tap ENTER. You now have three paragraphs.

6. Continue to Drill 5. Do not exit this document.

Serendipity, a new homework research tool from Information Technology Company, is available to subscribers of the major online services via the World Wide Web. Offered as a subscription service aimed at college students, Serendipity is a collection of tens of thousands of articles from major encyclopedias, reference books, magazines, pamphlets, and Internet sources combined into a single searchable database.

Serendipity puts an electronic library right at students' fingertips. The program offers two browse-and-search capabilities. Users can find articles by entering questions in simple question format or browse the database by pointing and clicking on key words that identify related articles. For more information, call 800.555.0174 or address email to lab@serendipity .com.

Lesson 11 Review

Warmup *Lesson 11a Warmup*

alphabet 1 Zeb had Jewel quickly give him five or six points.
" (quote) 2 Can you spell "chaos," "bias," "bye," and "their"?
y 3 Ty Clay may envy you for any zany plays you write.
easy 4 Did he bid on the bicycle, or did he bid on a map?

Skill Building

11b Improve Keystroking

> *Work for smoothness, not speed.*

5 za za zap az az maze zoo zip razz zed zax zoa zone
6 Liz Zahl saw Zoe feed the zebra in an Arizona zoo.

7 yj yj jy jy joy lay yaw say yes any yet my try you
8 Why do you say that today, Thursday, is my payday?

9 xs xs sax ox box fix hex ax lax fox taxi lox sixes
10 Roxy, you may ask Jay to fix any tax sets for you.

11 qa qa aqua quail quit quake quid equal quiet quart
12 Did Enrique quietly but quickly quell the quarrel?

13 fv fv five lives vow ova van eve avid vex vim void
14 Has Vivi, Vada, or Eva visited Vista Valley Farms?

11c Build Skill

> *Key balanced-hand words quickly and as phrases to increase speed.*

15 is to for do an may work so it but an with them am
16 am yam map aid zig yams ivy via vie quay cob amend

17 to do is for an may work so it but am an with them
18 for it|for it|to the|to the|do they|do they|do it

19 Pamela may go to the farm with Jan and a neighbor.
20 Rod and Ty may go by the lake if they go downtown.

Word Processing

Word Processor

You can use the Windows Word Processor in *KPDO* to practice keyboarding skills, create a letter, or take a timed writing. To access the Word Processor, click the button shown at the left. The Word Processor's formatting capabilities include:

- Fonts
- Styles
- Sizes

- Margins
- Tabs
- Justification

- Line Spacing
- Insert Pictures
- Insert Symbols
- Insert Tables

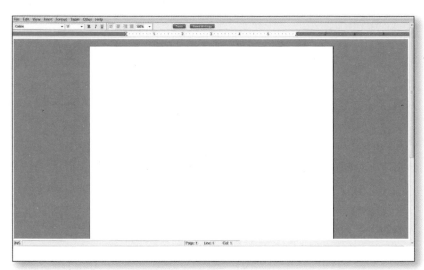

Note in Figure 1 that it is a *Windows* Word Processor, so it is similar to *Microsoft Word*.

Figure 1 Word Processor Open Screen

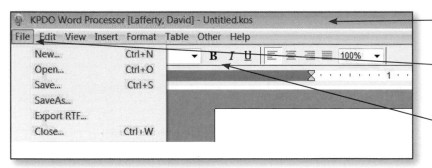

Figure 2 Ribbon and Menu of Commands

Title bar: Displays the name of the application and the document that is currently open.

Tabs: Each tab on the menu bar displays a menu of commands that you will use to create, edit, and format documents.

Toolbar: Provides shortcuts to many of the commands in the Word Processor.

Figure 3 Word Processor Timer

Timer: Click the Timer button on the Navigation bar at the top of the Word Processor screen to take a timed writing. Set the timer for 15" or 30" or for 1', 3', or 5'. The timing begins once you start to key and stops automatically.

11d Textbook Keying

Key each line once.

Key smoothly without looking at fingers.

```
       21  Make the return snappily
       22  and with assurance; keep
enter  23  your eyes on your source
       24  data; maintain a smooth,
       25  constant pace as you key.
```

When spacing, use a down-and-in motion.

```
space bar  26  us me it of he an by do go to us if or so am ah el
           27  To enter the website, key "Guest" as the password.
```

Press Caps Lock key to toggle on or off.

```
caps lock  28  Use ALL CAPS for items such as TO, FROM, or SUBJECT.
           29  Did Kristin mean Kansas City, MISSOURI, or KANSAS?
```

11e Timed Writing

1. Take two 1' timed writings. If you finish before time is up, begin again. The dot above words represents 2 *gwam*.
2. End the lesson.

Goal: 16 *gwam*

```
                                              wordwrap    gwam 1'  2'
              •            4            •            8
        Have we thought of communication as a kind      8   4
     •            12            •            16
 of war that we wage through each day?                  16   8
              •            4            •            8
        When we think of it that way, good language     24  12
     •            12            •            16            •
 would seem to become our major line of attack.         34  17
              •            4            •            8
        Words become muscle; in a normal exchange or in 43  22
  •            12            •            16            •            20
 a quarrel, we do well to realize the power of words.   53  27
```

11f Game

Use the game to showcase your skills.

11g Enrichment

1. Click the Skill Building tab from the main menu and choose Technique Builder; select Drill 1a.

2. Key Drill 1a from page 37. Key each line once, striving for good accuracy.

3. The results will be listed on the Skill Building Report.

TECHNIQUE TIP

Keep fingers curved and upright over home keys. Keep right thumb tucked under palm.

a	b	c	d	e	f
349	854	961	789	631	80
64	97	164	64	972	167
108	326	207	207	803	549
25	40	83	153	54	23
51	467	825	347	901	208
873	54	258	540	467	375
106	208	504	45	95	34
24	13	13	126	238	160
94	648	21	52	178	341
157	72	341	412	57	89
687	645	32	87	461	541
21	58	647	281	38	1,923
2,753	1,002	549	105	20	567
3,054	25	4,008	2,194	3,079	2,089
369	4,770	158	3,066	657	478
1,004	123	2,560	38	2,098	3,257
71.64	2.72	27.59	89.24	4.02	.57
285.36	118.50	438.96	102.46	55.71	6.37
3.79	24.73	4.71	527.90	.64	1.27
42.08	63.87	91.47	159.34	28.47	1.25
31.07	128.46	1.50	.28	374.95	116.00
365.87	.24	163.48	22.84	24.96	514.38
.25	394.28	452.87	349.51	852.43	234.94
147.25	32.54	821.47	164.87	.08	3.54
183.12	20.80	.60	5.07	121.07	.97

Lesson 12 Review

alphabet 1 Jack won five quiz games; Brad will play him next.

q 2 Quin Racq quickly and quietly quelled the quarrel.

z 3 Zaret zipped along sizzling, zigzag Arizona roads.

easy 4 Did he hang the sign by the big bush at the lake?

Skill Building

12b Improve Keystroking

b/f 5 bf bf fab fab ball bib rf rf rib rib fibs bums bee

6 Did Buffy remember that he is a brass band member?

z/y 7 za za zag zig zip yj yj jay eye day lazy hazy zest

8 Liz amazed us with the zesty pizza on a lazy trip.

q/u 9 qa qa quo qt. quit quay quad quarm que uj jug quay

10 Where is Quito? Qatar? Boqueirao? Quebec? Quilmes?

v/m 11 vf vf valve five value mj mj ham mad mull mass vim

12 Vito, enter the words vim, vivace, and avar; save.

all 13 I faced defeat; only reserves saved my best crews.

14 In my opinion, I need to rest in my reserved seat.

all 15 Holly created a red poppy and deserves art awards.

16 My pump averages a faster rate; we get better oil.

Keep fingers curved and body aligned properly.

12c Textbook Keying
Key each line once.

de/ed 17 ed fed led deed dell dead deal sled desk need seed

18 Dell dealt with the deed before the dire deadline.

ol/lo 19 old tolls doll solo look sole lost love cold stole

20 Old Ole looked for the long lost olive oil lotion.

op/po 21 pop top post rope pout port stop opal opera report

22 Stop to read the top opera opinion report to Opal.

we/ew 23 we few wet were went wears weather skews stew blew

24 Working women wear sweaters when weather dictates.

DRILL 4

Decimal

Follow the directions given. The decimal (.) key is usually located at the bottom right of the keypad. Use the third finger to reach down to tap the decimal key.

TECHNIQUE TIP

Tap each key with a quick, sharp stroke. Release the key quickly. Keep the fingers curved and upright, the wrist low and relaxed.

	a	b	c	d	e	f
	.28	.19	.37	.42	.81	.96
	.51	.67	.81	.27	.55	.80
	.64	.50	.60	.50	.62	.43
	7.10	8.91	5.64	3.12	6.04	5.01
	5.32	4.27	9.21	6.47	5.28	3.24
	8.94	3.06	7.38	5.89	1.37	6.78
	3.62	36.94	86.73	.60	8.21	4.02
	8.06	10.31	537.34	5.21	100.89	6.51
	321.04	10.55	687.52	164.84	.85	207.65
	.75	.26	10.85	627.98	2.57	46.51
	687.46	357.95	159.46	85.21	654.32	753.15
	20.46	220.48	6.10	3.04	123.54	315.47
	761.64	2.82	627.25	196.25	82.99	4.02
	285.46	34.60	.29	89.24	512.69	99.80
	33.99	739.45	290.23	563.21	701.21	546.78
	60.41	52.79	105.87	951.32	357.02	123.94
	108.97	211.00	46.24	82.47	61.28	75.61
	3.54	5.79	5.41	1.32	8.54	.27
	.05	1.19	77.54	112.96	33.68	2.75
	112.54	561.34	114.85	.24	647.21	432.89
	35.67	22.01	67.90	41.08	71.28	11.00
	579.21	105.24	731.98	258.96	741.21	546.21
	.34	1.68	.24	.87	.63	.54
	21.87	54.89	2.34	5.89	4.68	10.72

12d Textbook Keying

Key each line once.

25 a for we you is that be this will be a to and well
26 as our with I or a to by your form which all would
27 new year no order they so new but now year who may

28 This is Lyn's only date to visit their great city.
29 I can send it to your office at any time you wish.
30 She kept the fox, owls, and fowl down by the lake.

31 Harriette will cook dinner for the swimming teams.
32 Annette will call at noon to give us her comments.
33 Johnny was good at running and passing a football.

12e Timed Writing

1. Take a 2' timed writing. If you finish before time is up, begin again.
2. Use wordwrap.
3. End the lesson.

Goal: 16 *gwam*

Copy Difficulty

What factors determine whether copy is difficult or easy? Research shows that difficulty is influenced by syllables per word, characters per word, and percent of familiar words. Carefully controlling these three factors ensures that speed and accuracy scores are reliable—that is, increased scores reflect increased skill.

In Level 1, all timings are easy. Note "E" inside the triangle at left of the timing. Easy timings contain an average of 1.2 syllables per word, 5.1 characters per word, and 90 percent familiar words. Easy copy is suitable for the beginner who is mastering the keyboard.

	gwam	2'
There should be no questions, no doubt, about	5	35
the value of being able to key; it's just a matter	10	40
of common sense that today a pencil is much too slow.	15	45
Let me explain. Work is done on a keyboard	19	49
three to six times faster than other writing and	24	54
with a product that is a prize to read. Don't you	29	59
agree?	29	60

2' | 1 | 2 | 3 | 4 | 5 |

12f Enrichment

1. Click the Skill Building tab, and choose Technique Builder; select Drill 1b.
2. Key Drill 1b from page 37. Key each line once, striving for good accuracy.
3. The results will be listed on the Skill Building Report.
4. Log out of *KPDO*.

1, 2, 3

Complete Lesson 3 before keying Drill 3.

⭐ **TECHNIQUE TIP**

Keep fingers curved and upright over home keys. Keep right thumb tucked under palm.

© Cengage Learning

| 1 | 2 | 3 | 4 |

a	b	c	d	e	f
11	22	33	14	15	16
41	52	63	36	34	35
24	26	25	22	42	62
27	18	39	30	20	10
30	30	10	19	61	43
<u>32</u>	<u>31</u>	<u>21</u>	<u>53</u>	<u>83</u>	<u>71</u>
414	141	525	252	636	363
141	111	252	222	363	333
<u>111</u>	<u>414</u>	<u>222</u>	<u>525</u>	<u>333</u>	<u>636</u>
111	141	222	252	366	336
152	342	624	141	243	121
330	502	331	302	110	432
913	823	721	633	523	511
702	612	513	712	802	823
<u>213</u>	<u>293</u>	<u>821</u>	<u>813</u>	<u>422</u>	<u>722</u>
24	36	15	12	32	34
115	334	226	254	346	246
20	140	300	240	105	304
187	278	347	159	357	158
852	741	963	654	321	987
<u>303</u>	<u>505</u>	<u>819</u>	<u>37</u>	<u>92</u>	<u>10</u>
28	91	37	22	13	23
524	631	423	821	922	733
15	221	209	371	300	25
823	421	24	31	19	107
652	813	211	354	231	187
<u>50</u>	<u>31</u>	<u>352</u>	<u>16</u>	<u>210</u>	<u>30</u>

Lesson 13 Review

alphabet	1	Bev quickly hid two Japanese frogs in Mitzi's box.
shift	2	Jay Nadler, a Rotary Club member, wrote Mr. Coles.
, (comma)	3	Jay, Ed, and I paid for plates, knives, and forks.
easy	4	Did the amendment name a city auditor to the firm?

Skill Building

13b Textbook Keying
Key each line once.

Key short, familiar words as units.

5 is to for do an may work so it but an with them am
6 Did they mend the torn right half of their ensign?
7 Hand me the ivory tusk on the mantle by the bugle.

Key more difficult words by letter.

8 only state jolly zest oil verve join rate mop card
9 After defeat, look up; gaze in joy at a few stars.
10 We gazed at a plump beaver as it waded in my pool.

Use variable speed; your fingers will feel the difference.

11 it up so at for you may was but him work were they
12 It is up to you to get the best rate; do it right.
13 Sami greeted reporters as stars got ready at home.

13c Improve Keystroking

14 Pat appears happy to pay for any supper I prepare.
15 Knox can relax; Alex gets a box of flax next week.
16 Vi, Ava, and Viv move ivy vines, leaves, or stems.
17 It's a question of whether they can't or won't go.
18 Did Jane go? Did she see Sofia? Who paid? Did she?
19 Ms. E. K. Nu and Lt. B. A. Walz had the a.m. duty.
20 "Who are you?" he asked. "I am," I said, "Jayden."
21 Find a car; try it; like it; work a price; buy it.

DRILL 2

7, 8, 9

Complete Lesson 2 before keying Drill 2.

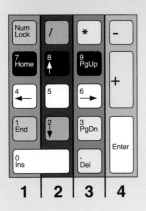

© Cengage Learning

| 1 | 2 | 3 | 4 |

a	b	c	d	e	f
74	85	96	70	80	90
47	58	96	87	78	98
90	70	80	90	90	70
89	98	78	89	77	87
86	67	57	48	68	57
59	47	48	67	58	69
470	580	690	770	707	407
999	969	888	858	474	777
777	474	888	585	999	696
858	969	747	770	880	990
757	858	959	857	747	678
579	849	879	697	854	796
857	967	864	749	864	795
609	507	607	889	990	448
597	847	449	457	684	599
85	74	96	98	78	88
957	478	857	994	677	579
657	947	479	76	94	795
887	965	789	577	649	849
90	80	70	806	709	407
407	567	494	97	80	70
50	790	807	90	75	968
408	97	66	480	857	57
87	479	567	947	808	970
690	85	798	587	907	89
94	754	879	67	594	847
489	880	97	907	69	579

13d Textbook Keying

Key each line once.

Keep hands and arms still as you reach up to the third row and down to the first row.

```
t 22  at fat hat sat to tip the that they fast last slat
r 23  or red try ran run air era fair rid ride trip trap
t/r 24  A trainer sprained an arm trying to tame the bear.

m 25  am me my mine jam man more most dome month minimum
n 26  no an now nine once net knee name ninth know never
m/n 27  Many men and women are important company managers.

o 28  on or to not now one oil toil over only solo today
i 29  it is in tie did fix his sit like with insist will
o/i 30  Joni will consider obtaining options to buy coins.

a 31  at an as art has and any case data haze tart smart
s 32  us as so say sat slap lass class just sassy simple
a/s 33  Disaster was averted as the steamer sailed to sea.

e 34  we he ear the key her hear chef desire where there
i 35  it is in tie did fix his sit like with insist will
e/i 36  An expression of gratitude for service is desired.
```

13e Timed Writing

1. Take two 2' timed writings. If you finish before time is up, begin again.
2. End the lesson; log out of *KPDO*.

Goal: 16 *gwam*

E ALL LETTERS

wordwrap   *gwam*   2'

```
      Some people think that the first impression made    5
in the first few seconds is the best method to find      10
out what a person is like. Think of meeting friends       15
for the first time. Was this true of them? In some        20
cases, one might be correct in judging a person in a      26
few seconds. However, in most cases, one will find        31
that it takes more than the first meeting to know         36
what a person is like. But the first time meeting a       41
person could give some idea, often if a person does       46
not show good qualities. For example, one might see       51
poor speaking skills, improper dress, and poor            56
personal traits when meeting a person for the first       61
time.                                                     62
```

2' | 1 | 2 | 3 | 4 | 5 |

4, 5, 6, 0

Complete Lesson 1 before keying Drill 1.

1. Turn on NUMLOCK. Click the Keypad Practice button.
2. Tap ENTER after each number.
3. To obtain a total, tap ENTER twice after the last number in a group.
4. Key each problem until the same answer is obtained twice; you can then be reasonably sure that you have the correct answer.

Follow these directions for each lesson.

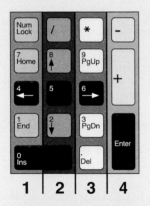

| 1 | 2 | 3 | 4 |

© Cengage Learning

a	b	c	d	e	f
46	55	56	46	55	56
45	64	45	45	64	45
66	56	64	66	56	64
56	44	65	56	44	65
54	65	45	54	65	45
65	54	44	65	54	44
466	445	546	654	465	665
564	654	465	545	446	645
456	464	546	545	564	456
556	544	644	466	644	646
644	455	464	654	464	554
454	546	565	554	456	656
400	404	505	606	500	600
404	505	606	500	600	400
500	600	400	404	505	606
650	506	404	550	440	550
506	460	605	460	604	640
406	500	640	504	460	560
504	640	550	440	660	406
560	450	650	450	505	550
640	504	440	640	450	660
400	600	500	500	600	400
650	505	404	606	540	560
504	404	640	404	406	606

Skill Builder 1

Skill Building *Technique Builder*

From the Skill Building tab, select Technique Builder and then the drill. Key each line once at a comfortable rate. Tap ENTER at the end of each line. Single-space the drill. Concentrate and key accurately. Repeat if desired.

DRILL 1

Goal: reinforce key locations

Key each line once at a comfortable, constant rate.

© Cengage Learning

★ TECHNIQUE TIP

Keep
- your eyes on source copy
- your fingers curved, upright
- your wrists low but not touching
- your elbows hanging loosely
- your feet flat on the floor

Drill 1a

A We saw that Alan had an alabaster vase in Alabama.
B My rubber boat bobbed about in the bubbling brook.
C Ceci gave cups of cold cocoa to Rebecca and Rocco.
D Don's dad added a second deck to his old building.
E Even as Ellen edited her document, she ate dinner.
F Our firm in Buffalo has a staff of forty or fifty.
G Ginger is giving Greg the eggs she got from Helga.
H Hugh has eighty high, harsh lights he might flash.

Drill 1b

I Irik's lack of initiative is irritating his coach.
J Judge J. J. Jore rejected Jeane and Jack's jargon.
K As a lark, Kirk kicked back a rock at Kim's kayak.
L Lucille is silly; she still likes lemon lollipops.
M Milt Mumm hammered a homer in the Miami home game.
N Ken Linn has gone hunting; Stan can begin canning.
O Jon Soto rode off to Otsego in an old Morgan auto.
P Philip helped pay the prize as my puppy hopped up.
Q Quiet Raquel quit quoting at an exquisite marquee.

Drill 1c

R As Mrs. Kerr's motor roared, her red horse reared.
S Sissie lives in Mississippi; Lissa lives in Tulsa.
T Nat told Betty not to tattle on her little sister.
U Ula has a unique but prudish idea on unused units.
V Eva visited every vivid event for twelve evenings.
W We watched as wayworn wasps swarmed by the willow.
X Tex Cox waxed the next box for Xenia and Rex Knox.
Y Ty says you may stay with Fay for only sixty days.
Z Hazel is puzzled about the azure haze; Zack dozes.

Skill Building

Keypad Lessons

Keypad instruction is available from the Keypad tab in *KPDO*. The NUMLOCK key must be on for you to use the software. The Summary Report shows the exercise you have completed and the scores achieved. Complete each lesson before keying the related practice on the next few pages.

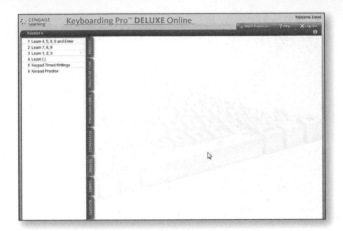

Keypad Timed Writings

Select Keypad Timed Writing on the Keypad lesson menu for additional keypad practice. Nine activities are available, each of which emphasizes a certain row or number type.

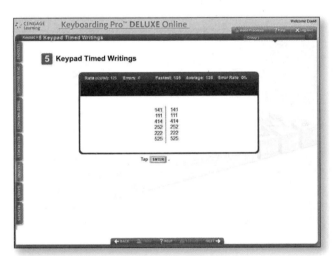

Keypad Practice

Select the Keypad Practice item to practice the exercises on the next few pages. Tap ENTER on the keypad after each number. Tap ENTER twice to sum the amounts keyed. Click the Print button to print the figures.

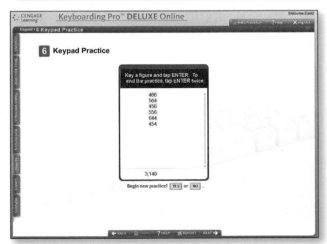

DRILL 2

Goal: strengthen up and down reaches

Keep hands and wrists quiet; fingers well curved in home position; stretch fingers up from home or pull them palmward as needed.

home position
1 Hall left for Dallas; he is glad Jake fed his dog.
2 Ada had a glass flask; Jake had a sad jello salad.
3 Lana Hask had a sale; Gala shall add half a glass.

down reaches
4 Did my banker, Mr. Mavann, analyze my tax account?
5 Do they, Mr. Zack, expect a number of brave women?
6 Zach, check the menu; next, beckon the lazy valet.

up reaches
7 Prue truly lost the quote we wrote for our report.
8 Teresa quietly put her whole heart into her words.
9 There were two hilarious jokes in your quiet talk.

DRILL 3

Goal: strengthen individual finger reaches

1st finger
1 Bob Mugho hunted for five minutes for your number.
2 Juan hit the bright green turf with his five iron.
3 The frigates and gunboats fought mightily in Java.

2nd finger
4 Dick said the ice on the creek had surely cracked.
5 Even as we picnicked, I decided we needed to diet.
6 Kim, not Mickey, had rice with chicken for dinner.

3rd/4th finger
7 Pam saw Roz wax an aqua auto as Lex sipped a cola.
8 Wally will quickly spell Zeus, Apollo, and Xerxes.
9 Who saw Polly? Pax Zais saw her; she is quiet now.

DRILL 4

Goal: strengthen special reaches

Emphasize smooth stroking. Avoid pauses, but do not reach for speed.

adjacent reaches
1 Falk knew well that her opinions of art were good.
2 Theresa answered her question; order was restored.
3 We join there and walk north to the western point.

direct reaches
4 Barb Nunn must hunt for my checks; she is in debt.
5 In June and December, Irvin hunts in Bryce Canyon.
6 We decided to carve a number of funny human faces.

double letters
7 Anne stopped off at school to see Bill Wiggs cook.
8 Edd has planned a small cookout for all the troop.
9 Keep adding to my assets all fees that will apply.

| 1 | 2 | 3 | 4 | 5 | 6 | 7 | 8 | 9 | 10 |

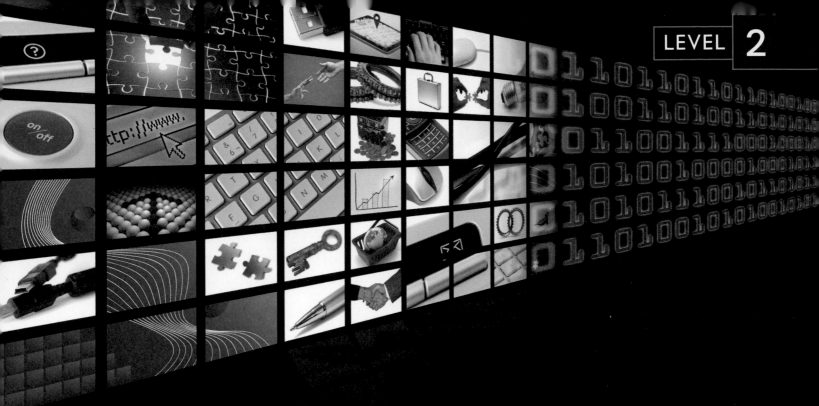

Applying Keyboarding Skill

Learning Outcomes

Numeric Keypad

+ To learn the numeric keypad by touch.

+ To develop fluency in using the keypad.

Word Processing Skills

+ To learn and apply basic word processing commands.

Communication Skills

+ To improve basic communication skills.

+ To develop proofreading and editing skills.

+ To compose and edit documents at the keyboard.

Web-Based Computing—Internet, Cloud, and Social Media

+ To search for and use Internet information efficiently.

+ To create and send effective emails.

+ To explore cloud computing and view and create documents using Web apps.

+ To explore social media tools.

Prepare for Your Future

+ To explore critical skills needed for career success.

+ To develop soft skills for career success through applications and a capstone project.

DRILL 5

Goal: improve troublesome pairs

Use a controlled rate without pauses.

```
       1  ad add did does dish down body dear dread dabs bad
  d/k  2  kid ok kiss tuck wick risk rocks kayaks corks buck
       3  Dirk asked Dick to kid Drake about the baked duck.

       4  deed deal den led heed made needs delay he she her
  e/i  5  kit kiss kiln kiwi kick kilt kind six ribs kill it
       6  Abie had neither ice cream nor fried rice in Erie.

       7  fib fob fab rib beg bug rob bad bar bed born table
  b/v  8  vat vet gave five ever envy never visit weave ever
       9  Vic and Bev gave five very big baby beds to a vet.

      10  aft after lift gift sit tot the them tax tutu tyro
  t/r 11  for far ere era risk rich rock rosy work were roof
      12  In Toronto, Ruth told the truth about her artwork.

      13  jug just jury judge juice unit hunt bonus quiz bug
  u/y 14  jay joy lay you your only envy quay oily whey body
      15  Willy usually does not buy your Yukon art in July.
```

DRILL 6

Goal: fluency

```
  1  Dian may make cocoa for the girls when they visit.
  2  Focus the lens for the right angle; fix the prism.
  3  She may suspend work when she signs the torn form.
  4  Augment their auto fuel in the keg by the autobus.
  5  As usual, their robot did half turns to the right.
  6  Pamela laughs as she signals to the big hairy dog.
  7  Pay Vivian to fix the island for the eighty ducks.
```

DRILL 7

Goal: eyes on the copy

Option: In the Word Processor, set the Timer for Variable and then either 20" or 30". Choose a *gwam* goal that is two to three words higher than your best rate. Try to reach your goal.

		words	30"	20"
1	Did she make this turkey dish? **ENTER**		12	18
2	Blake and Laurie may go to Dubuque.		14	21
3	Signal for the oak sleigh to turn right.		16	24
4	I blame Susie; did she quench the only flame?		18	27
5	She turns the panel dials to make this robot work.		20	30

LESSON E

Skill Building *Accuracy Emphasis*

Select the Skill Building tab; choose the appropriate emphasis and then Lesson E.

K P D O

Skill Building *Technique Builder*

DRILL 14

Word Beginnings

Key each line once, working for accuracy.

br
1 bright brown bramble bread breath breezes brought brother broiler
2 In February my brother brought brown bread and beans from Boston.

exe
3 exercises exert executives exemplify exemption executed exemplary
4 They exert extreme effort executing exercises in exemplary style.

bt
5 doubt subtle obtains obtrusion subtracts indebtedness undoubtedly
6 Extreme debt will cause more than subtle doubt among my creditors.

ny
7 tiny funny company nymph penny nylon many anyone phony any brainy
8 Anyone as brainy and funny as Penny is an asset to their company.

K P D O

Timed Writings

1. Take a 1' writing on each paragraph.
2. Take a 3' writing on both paragraphs.

Writing 27

gwam 1' | 3'

Many people believe that an ounce of prevention is worth a pound   14 | 5
of cure. Care of your heart can help you prevent serious physical   27 | 9
problems. The human heart is the most important pump ever   39 | 13
developed. It constantly pushes blood through the body tissues. But   52 | 17
the layers of muscle that make up the heart must be kept in proper   66 | 22
working order. Exercise can help this muscle to remain in good   78 | 26
condition.   80 | 27

Another important way to maintain a healthy heart is just by   13 | 31
avoiding habits which are considered to be greatly detrimental to the   27 | 36
body. Food that is high in cholesterol is not a good choice. Also,   41 | 40
use of tobacco has quite a negative effect on the function of the   54 | 49
heart. You can minimize your chances of heart problems by avoiding   67 | 54
these bad health habits.   72 | 55

| 1' | 1 | 2 | 3 | 4 | 5 | 6 | 7 | 8 | 9 | 10 | 11 | 12 | 13 |
| 3' | | 1 | | 2 | | | 3 | | | 4 | | | |

Timed Writings

Any timed writing in the book can be completed using the Timed Writing feature.

TO USE THE TIMED WRITING FEATURE:

1. From the Timed Writings tab, select the timed writing.
2. Select the source and the timing length. For example,
   - Select Paragraph 1 and 1'. Key paragraph 1; if you finish before time is up, repeat the same paragraph. Always use wordwrap when keying timed writings.
   - Select Paragraph 2 and 1'. Key paragraph 2; repeat the same paragraph if you finish before time is up.
   - Select Entire Writing and 2'. Try to maintain your 1' rate. If you finish before time is up, start over, beginning with paragraph 1.
3. Timings save automatically.
4. The Timed Writing Report displays the results of the last 40 timed writings and the best 3 timings at each timing length (1', 2', 3').

wordwrap

Goal: build staying power

1. Key each paragraph as a 1' timing. Use wordwrap.
2. Key a 2' timing on both paragraphs. Use wordwrap.

Writing 1: 18 *gwam* gwam 2'

Why spend weeks with some problem when just a few quiet   6
minutes can help us to resolve it.   9

If we don't take time to think through a problem, it will   15
swiftly begin to expand in size.   18

Writing 2: 20 *gwam*

We push very hard in our quest for growth, and we all think   6
that only excellent growth will pay off.   10

Believe it or not, one can actually work much too hard,   16
be much too zealous, and just miss the mark.   20

Writing 3: 22 *gwam*

A business friend once explained to me why he was often   6
quite eager to be given some new project to work with.   11

My friend said that each new project means he has to   16
organize and use the best of his knowledge and his skill.   22

Writing 4: 24 *gwam*

Just don't let new words get away from you. Learn how to spell   6
and pronounce new words and when and how to use them with skill.   13

A new word is a friend, but frequently more. New words   19
must be used lavishly to extend the size of your word power.   25

2' | 1 | 2 | 3 | 4 | 5 | 6 |

LESSON D

Skill Building *Accuracy Emphasis*

Select the Skill Building tab; choose the appropriate emphasis and then Lesson D.

Skill Building *Technique Builder*

DRILL 13

Adjacent Key Review

Key each line once; strive for accuracy.

1 nm many enmity solemn kl inkling weekly pickle oi oil invoice join
2 iu stadium medium genius lk milk talk walks uy buy buyer soliloquy
3 mn alumni hymn number column sd Thursday wisdom df mindful handful
4 me mention comment same fo found perform info le letter flew files

5 The buyer sent his weekly invoices for oil to the group on Thursday.
6 Mindful of the alumni, the choirs sang a hymn prior to my soliloquy.
7 An inmate, a fogger, and a genius joined the weekly talks on Monday.
8 They were to join in the talk shows to assess regions of the Yukon.

Timed Writings

1. Take a 1' writing on each paragraph.
2. Take a 3' writing on both paragraphs.

Writing 26

gwam 1' | 3'

All people, in spite of their eating habits, have two major needs   13 | 4
that must be met by their food. They need food that provides a   26 | 9
source of energy, and they need food that will fill the skeletal and   40 | 13
operating needs of their bodies. Carbohydrates, fats, and protein   53 | 18
form a major portion of the diet. Vitamins and minerals are also   66 | 22
necessary for excellent health.   72 | 24

Carbohydrates make up a major source of our energy needs.   12 | 28
Fats also serve as a source of energy and act as defense against   25 | 32
cold and trauma. Proteins are changed to amino acids, which are   38 | 37
the building units of the body. These, in turn, are utilized to make   52 | 41
most body tissue. Minerals are required to control many body   64 | 45
functions, and vitamins are used for normal growth and aid against   77 | 50
disease.   84 | 52

1' | 1 | 2 | 3 | 4 | 5 | 6 | 7 | 8 | 9 | 10 | 11 | 12 | 13 |
3' | 1 | 2 | 3 | 4 |

Writing 5: 26 *gwam*

gwam 2'

We usually get the best results when we know where 5

we are going. Just setting a few goals will help us quietly 12

see what we can do. 13

Goals can help measure whether we are moving at a good 19

rate or dozing along. You can expect a goal to help you find 25

good results. 26

Writing 6: 28 *gwam*

To win whatever prizes we want from life, we must plan to 6

move carefully from this goal to the next to get the maximum 12

result from our work. 14

If we really want to become skilled in keying, we must 19

come to see that this desire will require of us just a little 26

patience and hard work. 28

Writing 7: 30 *gwam*

Am I an individual person? I'm sure I am; still, in a 5

much, much bigger sense, other people have a strong voice in 12

thoughts I think and actions I take. 15

Although we are each a unique person, we work and 21

play in organized groups of people who just do not expect us to 26

dismiss their rules of law and order. 30

2' | 1 | 2 | 3 | 4 | 5 | 6 |

LESSON C

Skill Building *Accuracy Emphasis*

Select the Skill Building tab, the appropriate emphasis, and then Lesson C. Your results will be summarized in the Skill Building Report.

Skill Building *Technique Builder*

DRILL 12

Balanced-Hand

Key each line once for fluency.

1 an anyone brand spans th their father eighth he head sheets niche
2 en enters depends been nd end handle fund or original sport color
3 ur urban turns assure to took factory photo ti titles satin still
4 ic ice bicycle chic it item position profit ng angle danger doing

5 I want the info in the file on the profits from the chic bicycle.
6 Hang the sign by the lake not by an island by six or eight today.
7 Did Vivian, the widow, pay for eight flair pens, and eight gowns?
8 When did Viviana go to the firm to sign the title to the emblems?

Timed Writings

1. Take a 1' writing on each paragraph.
2. Take a 3' writing on both paragraphs.

Writing 25

gwam 1' | 3'

Practicing basic health rules will result in good body condition. 14 | 5
Proper diet is a way to achieve good health. Eat a variety of foods each 29 | 10
day, including some fruit, vegetables, cereal products, and foods rich 43 | 14
in protein, to be sure that you keep a balance. Another part of a good 57 | 19
health plan is physical activity, such as running. 67 | 22

Running has become quite popular in this country. Some people 13 | 27
run for the joy of running, others run because they want to maximize 27 | 31
the benefits that can be gained by running on a regular basis. Some 41 | 36
of the benefits include weight loss, improved heart health, improved 55 | 41
bone health, and improved mood. Running is one of the most effective 68 | 45
forms of exercise that will help achieve ideal body weight. 80 | 49

1' | 1 | 2 | 3 | 4 | 5 | 6 | 7 | 8 | 9 | 10 | 11 | 12 | 13 |
3' | 1 | 2 | 3 | 4 |

Figure and Symbol Keys

LEARNING OUTCOMES

- Key the numeric keys by touch.
- Use symbol keys correctly.
- Build keying speed and accuracy.
- Apply correct number expression.
- Apply proofreaders' marks.

Lesson 14   l and 8

K P D O

Warmup   *Lesson 14a Warmup*

New Keys

14b   1 and 8

1 Reach *up* with *left fourth* finger.

8 Reach *up* with *right second* finger.

14c   All Figures Learned

Abbreviations: Do not space after a period within an abbreviation, as in Ph.D., U.S., C.O.D., a.m.

The digit "1" and the letter "l" have separate values; do not interchange.

1

1   1 1a a1 1 1; 1 and a 1; 1 add 1; 1 aunt; 1 ace; 1 arm; 1 aye
2   1 and 11 and 111; 11 eggs; 11 vats; Set 11A; May 11; Item 11
3   The 11 aces of the 111th Corps each rated a salute at 1 p.m.

8

4   8 8k k8 8 8; 8 kits; ask 8; 8 kites; kick 8; 8 keys; spark 8
5   OK 88; 8 bags; 8 or 88; the 88th; 88 kegs; ask 88; order 888
6   Eight of the 88 cars score 8 or better on our Form 8 rating.
7   She did live at 818 Park, not 181 Park; or was it 181 Clark?
8   Put 1 with 8 to form 18; put 8 with 1 to write 81. Use 1881.
9   On May 1 at 8 a.m., 18 men and 18 women left Gate 8 for Rio.

LESSON B

Skill Building *Accuracy Emphasis*

1. Select the Skill Building tab and choose either Speed Emphasis or Accuracy Emphasis as recommended in Assessment 1. Complete Lesson B.

2. Your results will be summarized in the Skill Building Report.

Skill Building *Technique Builder*

DRILL 11

Balanced-Hand

Key each line once, working for fluency.

1 to today stocks into ti times sitting until ur urges further tour
2 en entire trend dozen or order support editor nd and mandate land
3 he healthy check ache th these brother both an annual change plan
4 nt into continue want of office softer roof is issue poison basis

5 Did Pamela sign the title to the big lake mansion by Lamb Island?
6 Rick is to pay the eight men and women if they do the work right.
7 My time for a land bus tour will not change until further notice.
8 I am to blame for the big problem with the maid; I can handle it.

Timed Writings

1. Key a 1' writing on each paragraph. Compare your *gwam*.

2. Key additional 1' writings on the slower paragraph.

Writing 24

gwam 1' | 3'

Most of us have, at some time or another, recognized an annoying   14 | 5

problem and had valid reasons to complain. The complaint may have   27 | 9

been because of a defective product, poor customer services, or   40 | 13

perhaps growing tired of talking to voice mail. However, many of us   54 | 18

feel that complaining to a business firm is an exercise in futility   67 | 22

so we do not bother. Instead, we just remain quiet, write it off as a   81 | 27

bad experience and continue to be taken advantage of.   92 | 31

Today, more than at any time in the past consumers are taking some   13 | 35

steps to let their feelings be known—and with a great amount of   26 | 39

success. As a result, firms are becoming more responsive to   38 | 43

the needs of the consumer. complaints from customers alert firms   51 | 48

to produce or service defect and there by cause action to be taken   64 | 52

for their benefit.   68 | 53

1'	1	2	3	4	5	6	7	8	9	10	11	12	13
3'		1			2			3			4		

Skill Building

14d Textbook Keying

Key each line once.

Work for fluency as you key these high-frequency words.

10 a an it been copy for his this more no office please service
11 our service than the they up was work all any many thank had
12 business from I know made more not me new of some to program
13 such these two with your about and have like department year
14 by at on but do had in letter most now one please you should
15 their order like also appreciate that there gentlemen letter
16 be can each had information letter may make now only so that
17 them time use which am other been send to enclosed have will
18 Please thank the department staff for the excellent program.
19 Therefore, send the information as they are very interested.
20 She sent a receipt and an invoice for the payment due today.
21 Our board and president are happy about the new tax service.
22 We appreciate the excellent help received from every office.
23 Please return the attached form prior to the second meeting.

14e Improve Keystroking

figures

24 Our 188 trucks moved 1881 tons on August 18 and December 18.
25 Send Mary 181 No. 188 panes for her home at 8118 Oak Street.
26 The 188 men in 8 boats left Docks 1 and 18 at 1 p.m., May 1.
27 pop was lap pass slaw wool solo swap Apollo wasp load plaque
28 Was Polly acquainted with the skillful jazz player in Texas?
29 The computer is a useful tool; it helps you to perform well.

30 Did their form entitle them to the land?
31 Did the men in the field signal for us to go?
32 I may pay for the antique bowls when I go to town.
33 The auditor did the work right, so he risks no penalty.
34 The man by the big bush did signal us to turn down the lane.

14f Enrichment

1. Key these lines in the game.
2. Log out of *KPDO* when completed.

Skill Builder 3

LESSON A

K P D O

Skill Building *Accuracy Emphasis*

1. Select the Skill Building tab, Accuracy Emphasis, and then Assessment 1.

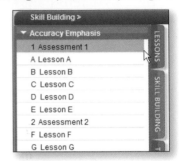

2. Key the timing from the screen for 3'; work for control.

3. Complete Lesson A or the first lesson you have not completed in either Speed Emphasis or Accuracy Emphasis as suggested by the software.

4. Your results will be summarized in the Skill Building Report.

K P D O

Timed Writings

Writing 23

1. Key a 1' writing on each paragraph. (Remember to change the source in the Timed Writing Settings dialog box.) Compare your *gwam* on the two paragraphs.

2. Key additional 1' writings on the slower paragraph.

	gwam	1'	3'
The most valuable employees stand a greater chance of		11	4
maintaining their job in hard economic times. There are many		23	8
qualities which distinguish an excellent employee from other workers.		37	12
In the first place, they remain focused and keep their minds on the		51	17
tasks at hand. Good employees think about the work they perform and		64	21
how it relates to the total success of the project. They act as team		78	26
leaders and guide the project to completion.		87	29
Second, good workers have the ability to work consistently and		14	33
fully realize every goal. Many people in the workplace perform just		27	38
bits and pieces of a job. They begin one thing, but allow themselves		41	42
to be quickly distracted from the work at hand. Many people are good		55	47
starters, but fewer are also good finishers.		64	50

```
1'| 1 | 2 | 3 | 4 | 5 | 6 | 7 | 8 | 9 | 10 | 11 | 12 | 13 |
3'|     1     |     2     |     3     |     4     |
```

Lesson 15 5 and 0

New Keys

15b 5 and 0

5 Reach *up* with *left first* finger.

0 Reach *up* with *right fourth* finger.

5

1 5 5f f5 5 5; 5 fans; 5 feet; 5 figs; 5 fobs; 5 frus; 5 flaws
2 5 o'clock; 5 a.m.; 5 p.m.; is 55 or less; buy 55; 5 and 5 is
3 Call Line 555 if 5 fans or 5 bins arrive at Pier 5 by 5 p.m.

0

4 0 0; ;0 0 0; skip 0; plan 0; left 0; is below 0; I scored 0;
5 0 degrees; key 0 and 0; write 00 here; the total is 0 or 00;
6 She laughed at their 0 to 0 score; but ours was 0 to 0 also.

15c All Figures Learned

7 I keyed 550 pages for Invoice 05, or 50 more than we needed.
8 Pages 15 and 18 of the program listed 150, not 180, members.
9 On May 10, Rick drove 500 miles to New Mexico in car No. 08.

Skill Building

15d Textbook Keying

Key each line once.

Watch the copy, not the hands.

10 Read pages 5 and 8; duplicate page 18; omit pages 50 and 51.
11 We have Model 80 with 10 meters or Model 180 with 15 meters.
12 After May 18, French 050 meets in room 15 at 10 a.m. daily.

13 Barb Abver saw a vibrant version of her brave venture on TV.
14 Call a woman or a man who will manage Minerva Manor in Nome.
15 We were quick to squirt a quantity of water at Quin and West.

Writing 20

	1'	3'

If asked, most people will agree that some people have far more creative skills than others, and they will also say that these skills are in great demand by most organizations. A follow-up question is in order. Are you born with creative skills or can you develop them? There is no easy answer to that question, but it is worth spending a good bit of time pondering.

	1'	3'
	13	4
	25	8
	38	13
	52	17
	64	21
	74	25

If creative skills can be developed, then the next issue is how can you develop these skills. One way is to approach each task with a determination to solve the problem and a refusal to accept failure. If the normal way of doing a job does not work, just keep trying things never tried before until you reach a good solution. This is called thinking outside the box.

	1'	3'
	13	29
	25	33
	38	37
	50	41
	63	46
	73	49

1' | 1 | 2 | 3 | 4 | 5 | 6 | 7 | 8 | 9 | 10 | 11 | 12 | 13 |
3' | | 1 | | 2 | | 3 | | 4 |

Writing 21

Figures are not as easy to key as many of the words we use. Balanced-hand figures such as 16, 27, 38, 49, and 50, although fairly easy, are slower to key because each one requires longer reaches and uses more time per stroke.

	1'	3'
	12	4
	24	8
	37	12
	44	15

Figures such as 12, 45, 67, and 90 are even more difficult because they are next to one another and each uses just a single hand to key. Because of their size, bigger numbers such as 178, 349, and 1,220 create extra speed losses.

	1'	3'
	12	19
	24	23
	37	27
	45	30

1' | 1 | 2 | 3 | 4 | 5 | 6 | 7 | 8 | 9 | 10 | 11 | 12 | 13 |
3' | | 1 | | 2 | | 3 | | 4 |

Skill Transfer

1. Set the Timer for 2'. Take a 2' writing on paragraph 1.

2. Set the Timer for 2'. Take a 2' writing on paragraph 2.

3. Take 2 or more 2' writings on the slower paragraph.

Writing 22

Few people are able to attain financial success without some kind of planning. People who realize the value of wise spending and saving are those who set up a budget. A budget will help them to determine just how much they can spend and how much they can save so that they will not squander their money recklessly.

	1'	2'
	13	7
	25	13
	38	19
	49	25
	62	31

Keeping records is a ~~crucial~~ *vital* part of a budget. Complete *ing* A detailed records of all income and expenses *ditures* over a period of a ~~number of~~ *several* months *will* can help to determine what bills, ~~as water~~ *like utilities* or rent, are *fixed* ~~static~~ and which are flexible. To get the most out of your income, *focus on* pay attention to the items that you can ~~modify~~ *be changed*.

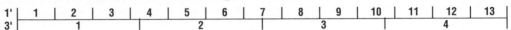

	1'	2'
	11	37
	23	42
	35	49
	47	54
	58	60

1' | 1 | 2 | 3 | 4 | 5 | 6 | 7 | 8 | 9 | 10 | 11 | 12 |
2' | | 1 | | 2 | | 3 | | 4 | | 5 | | 6 |

15e Textbook Keying

Key each line once.

pu/nv

16 pumps impulse campus invoices convey envy puck public canvas
17 Computer's input on environmental canvass confirms decision.

mb ey rk

18 embarked number climb eye obeying park remark thumb attorney
19 Ambitious people gambled money on unusual pieces of artwork.

tl ru pt

20 subtle apt capture excerpt adult abrupt brittle forums drug
21 Ruth opts to be greatly optimistic about seven new recruits.

ob rg un

22 objective lobster organize urge bounce tribunal global surge
23 Marge's hunger for mobile action targets frequent traveling.

15f Timed Writing

1. Take two 1' timed writings. If you finish before time is up, begin again.
2. Use wordwrap; do not tap ENTER at the end of lines.
3. End the lesson.

LA ALL LETTERS

wordwrap ↓

gwam 1'

I thought about Harry and how he worked for me in my   11
family insurance business for 10 years; how daily at 8 he   23
parked his old car in the company lot; then, he left exactly   35
at 5. Every day was almost identical for him.   44
In a quiet way, he did an outstanding job, requesting   56
little attention. So I never recognized his thirst for travel.   68
I didn't expect to find all those travel brochures near his   80
workplace.   82

1' | 1 | 2 | 3 | 4 | 5 | 6 | 7 | 8 | 9 | 10 | 11 | 12 |

Communication

15g Enrichment

Word Processor

1. Go to the Word Processor.
2. Compose one paragraph that describes travel that you have done or perhaps that you wish to take. Include at least two attractions you visited or hope to visit while on this trip. Use proper grammatical structure. Do not worry about keying errors at this time.
3. Save the document as *xx-travel*. (Replace *xx* with your initials.)
4. Log out of *KPDO*.

Writing 17

gwam 1' | 3'

Many people like to say just how lucky or fortunate a person   13 | 4
is when he or she succeeds in doing something extremely well. Does   26 | 9
luck play a significant part in success? In some cases, it might have a   40 | 13
small effect.   43 | 14

Being in the right place at the right time may help, but hard   13 | 19
work may produce far greater results than luck. Those who simply   26 | 23
wait for luck should not expect immediate or quick results and   39 | 27
should realize luck may never come.   46 | 30

```
1' | 1 | 2 | 3 | 4 | 5 | 6 | 7 | 8 | 9 | 10 | 11 | 12 |
3' |     1     |     2     |     3     |     4     |
```

Writing 18

gwam 1' | 3'

New golfers must learn to zero in on several social rules. Do   12 | 4
not engage in conversation, stand close, or move around when   24 | 8
another person is hitting. Be prepared to play when it is your turn.   38 | 13

Always take practice swings in an area away from other   11 | 16
people. Do not rest on your club on the green when waiting your turn.   25 | 21
Proper etiquette requires you to let the group behind you play through   39 | 25
if your group is slow.   43 | 27

Set your other clubs down off the green. Leave the green   11 | 31
quickly when you have finished; update your card on the next tee.   24 | 35
Always leave the course in good condition for others to enjoy.   37 | 39
Good sportsmanship is just as important as having a good time.   49 | 43

```
1' | 1 | 2 | 3 | 4 | 5 | 6 | 7 | 8 | 9 | 10 | 11 | 12 |
3' |     1     |     2     |     3     |     4     |
```

Writing 19

gwam 1' | 3'

Do you know how to utilize time wisely? If you do, then its   12 | 4
appropriate use can help you organize and run a business better. If   25 | 8
you find that your daily problems tend to keep you from planning   38 | 13
properly, then perhaps you are not utilizing time well. You may find   52 | 17
that you spend too much time on tasks that are not important. Plan   65 | 22
your work to save valuable time.   71 | 24

A firm that does not plan is liable to experience trouble. A   12 | 28
small firm may have difficulty planning. It is important to know just   26 | 32
where the firm is headed. A firm may have a fear of learning things it   40 | 37
would rather not know. To say that planning is easy would be absurd.   54 | 42
It requires a significant amount of thinking and planning to meet the   67 | 46
expectations of the firm.   72 | 48

```
1' | 1 | 2 | 3 | 4 | 5 | 6 | 7 | 8 | 9 | 10 | 11 | 12 |
3' |     1     |     2     |     3     |     4     |
```

Lesson 16 2 and 7

New Keys

16b 2 and 7

2 Reach *up* with *left third* finger.

7 Reach *up* with *right first* finger.

2

1 2 2s s2 2 2; has 2 sons; is 2 sizes; was 2 sites; has 2 skis
2 add 2 and 2; 2 sets of 2; catch 22; as 2 of the 22; 222 Main
3 Exactly at 2 on April 22, the 22nd Company left from Pier 2.

7

4 7 7j j7 7 7; 7 jets; 7 jeans; 7 jays; 7 jobs; 7 jars; 7 jaws
5 ask for 7; buy 7; 77 years; June 7; take any 7; deny 77 boys
6 From May 7 on, all 77 men will live at 777 East 77th Street.

16c All Figures Learned

7 I read 2 of the 72 books, Ellis read 7, and Han read all 72.
8 Tract 27 cites the date as 1850; Tract 170 says it was 1852.
9 You can take Flight 850 on January 12; I'll take Flight 705.

Skill Building

16d Textbook Keying

Key each line once. Keep fingers curved and relaxed; wrists low.

3rd/4th
10 pop was lap pass slaw wool solo swap apollo wasp load plaque
11 Al's quote was, "I was dazzled by the jazz, pizza, and pool."

1st/2nd
12 bad fun nut kick dried night brick civic thick hutch believe
13 Kim may visit her friends in Germany if I give her a ticket.

3rd/1st
14 cry tube wine quit very curb exit crime ebony mention excite
15 To be invited, petition the six executive committee members.

Writing 14

What do you expect when you have the opportunity to travel to a foreign country? Quite a few people realize that one of the real joys of traveling is to get a brief, but revealing glimpse of how foreigners think, work, and live.

The best way to enjoy a different culture is to learn as much about the country being visited and its culture as you can before you leave home. Then you can concentrate on being an informed guest rather than trying to find local people who can meet your needs.

	1'	3'
	12	4
	26	9
	39	13
	45	15
	12	19
	26	24
	39	28
	52	32

Writing 15

What do you enjoy doing in your free time? Health experts tell us that far too many people choose to be lazy rather than to be active. The unpleasant result of that misguided decision shows up in our weight.

Working to control what we weigh is difficult, and seldom can it be accomplished quickly. However, it is extremely important if our weight exceeds what it should be. Part of the problem results from the amount and type of food we eat.

If we desire to appear fit, we should include exercise as a substantial component of our weight loss program. Walking at least thirty minutes each day at a very fast rate can make a major difference in our appearance and in the way we feel.

	1'	3'
	13	4
	25	8
	39	13
	41	14
	12	18
	26	22
	39	27
	46	29
	12	33
	25	37
	37	41
	48	45

Writing 16

Doing what we enjoy doing is quite important; however, enjoying what we have to do is equally important. As you ponder both of these concepts, you may feel that they are the same, but they are quite different.

If we could do only those things that we prefer to do, the chances are that we would do them exceptionally well. Generally, we will take more pride in doing those things we thoroughly enjoy doing, and we will not stop until we get them done correctly.

We realize, though, that we cannot restrict the tasks and responsibilities that we must do just to those that we prefer to do. Therefore, we need to build an interest in and an appreciation of all the tasks that we must do in our positions.

	1'	3'
	11	4
	23	8
	37	12
	41	14
	12	18
	26	22
	37	26
	50	30
	11	34
	25	39
	39	43
	48	46

1'	1	2	3	4	5	6	7	8	9	10	11	12
3'		1			2			3			4	

16e Improve Keystroking

16 line 8; Book 1; No. 88; Seat 11; June 18; Cart 81; date 1881

17 take 2; July 7; buy 22; sell 77; mark 27; adds 72; Memo 2772

18 feed 5; bats 0; age 50; Ext. 55; File 50; 55 bags; band 5005

19 I work 18 visual signs with 20 turns of the 57 lenses to 70.

20 Did 17 boys fix the gears for 50 bicycles in 28 racks or 10?

16f Textbook Keying

Key each line once.

> *Think and key the words and phrases as units rather than letter by letter.*

words: *think, say, and key words*

21 is do am lay cut pen dub may fob ale rap cot hay pay hem box

22 box wit man sir fish also hair giant rigor civic virus ivory

23 laugh sight flame audit formal social turkey bicycle problem

phrases: *think, say, and key phrases*

24 is it│is it│if it is│if it is│or by│or by│or me│or me│for us

25 and all│for pay│pay dues and│the pen│the pen box│the pen box

26 such forms│held both│work form│then wish│sign name│with them

easy sentences

27 The man is to do the work right; he then pays the neighbors.

28 Sign the forms to pay the eight men for the turkey and hams.

29 The antique ivory bicycle is a social problem for the chair.

16g Timed Writing

1. Take two 2' timed writings. If you finish before time is up, begin again. Use wordwrap.

2. End the lesson; log out of *KPDO*.

Goal: 16 *gwam*

gwam 2' | 3'

When choosing a password, do not select one you have   6 | 4
already used. Create a new one quite often, perhaps every   11 | 8
three to four weeks. Be sure to use a combination of both   17 | 11
letters and numbers.   19 | 13

Know your password; do not record it on paper. If you   25 | 17
must write it down, be sure the password is not recognized.   31 | 21
Don't let anyone watch you key. Just position yourself away   37 | 24
from the person or key a few extra strokes.   41 | 27

2' | 1   2   3   4   5   6
3' | 1   2   3   4

Writing 11

gwam 3'

Anyone who expects some day to find a great job should   4
begin now to learn the value of accuracy. To be worth anything,   8
final work must be correct, without question. Of course, we   12
realize that the human aspect of the work equation always raises   16
the chance of errors; but we should understand that those same   20
errors can be found and fixed. Every completed job should carry   24
at least one stamp; the stamp of true pride in work that is exemplary.   29

Writing 12

No question about it: Many of the personal problems we face   4
today arise from the fact that we have never been very wise   8
consumers. We have not used our natural resources well; as a result,   13
we have jeopardized much of our environment. We excused our   17
actions because we thought that our stock of most resources had no   21
limit at all. So, at last, we are beginning to realize just how indiscreet   26
we were; and we are taking steps to rebuild our world.   30

Writing 13

When I see people in top jobs, I know I am seeing people who   4
sell. I am not just referring to employees who work in a retail outlet; I   9
mean all people who put extra effort into convincing others to   13
recognize their best qualities. They, themselves, are what they sell;   18
and the major tools they use are their appearance, their language, and   22
their personality. They look great, they talk and write well; and, with   27
much self-confidence, they meet you eye to eye.   30

3' | 1 | 2 | 3 | 4 |

Lesson 17 4 and 9

Warmup *Lesson 17a Warmup*

New Keys

17b 4 and 9

4 Reach *up* with *left first* finger.

9 Reach *up* with *right third* finger.

4

1 4 4f f4 f f f; if 4 furs; off 4 floors; gaff 4 fish; 4 flags
2 44th floor; half of 44; 4 walked 44 flights; 4 girls; 4 boys
3 I order exactly 44 bagels, 4 cakes, and 4 pies before 4 a.m.

9

4 9 9l l9 9 9 9; fill 9 lugs; call 9 lads; Bill 9 lost; dial 9
5 also 9 oaks; roll 9 loaves; 9.9 degrees; sell 9 oaks; Hall 9
6 Just 9 couples, 9 men and 9 women, left at 9 on our Tour 99.

17c All Figures Learned

7 4 feet; 4 inches; 44 gallons, 444 quarts, 4 folders, 44 fads
8 Lucky 99; 999 leaves; 9 lottery tickets; 9 losers; 9 winners
9 Memo 94 says 9 pads, 4 pens, and 4 ribbons were sent July 9.
10 Study Item 17 and Item 28 on page 40 and Item 59 on page 49.
11 Within 17 months he drove 85 miles, walked 29, and flew 490.

Skill Building

17d Textbook Keying

Key each line once.

Keep hands quiet as you reach to the top row; do not bounce.

12 My staff of *18* worked *11* hours a day from May *27* to June *12*.
13 There were *5* items tested by Inspector *7* at *4* p.m. on May *8*.
14 Please send her File *10* today at *8*; her access number is *97*.
15 Car *947* had its trial run. The qualifying speed was *198* mph.
16 The estimated total score? *485*. Actual? *390*. Difference? *95*.

Assess Skill Growth:

1. Select the Timed Writings tab from the Main menu.
2. Select the writing number such as Writing 8.
3. Select 3' as the length of the writing. Use wordwrap.
4. Repeat the timing if desired.

Word Processor Option:

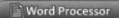 Word Processor

1. Key 1' writings on each paragraph of a timing. Note that paragraphs within a timing increase by two words.
   Goal: to complete each paragraph
2. Key a 3' timing on the entire writing.

gwam
1' | 3'

Writing 8

	1'	3'
Any of us whose target is to have success in our professional	12	4
work will understand that we must learn how to work in harmony	25	8
with others whose paths may cross ours daily.	34	11
We will, unquestionably, work for, with, and beside people, just	13	15
as they will work for, with, and beside us. We will judge them,	25	20
as most certainly they are going to be judging us.	35	23
A lot of people realize the need for solid working relations and	13	27
have a rule that treats others as they, themselves, expect to be	26	32
treated. This seems to be a sound, practical idea for them.	37	35

Writing 9

	1'	3'
I spoke with one company visitor recently; and she was very much	13	4
impressed, she said, with the large amount of work she had noted	26	9
being finished by one of our front office workers.	36	12
I told her how we had just last week recognized this very person	13	16
for what he had done, for output, naturally, but also because of	26	21
its excellence. We know this person has that "magic touch."	38	25
This "magic touch" is the ability to do a fair amount of work in	13	29
a fair amount of time. It involves a desire to become ever more	26	34
efficient without losing quality--the "touch" all workers should	39	38
have.	40	38

Writing 10

	1'	3'
Isn't it great just to untangle and relax after you have keyed a	13	4
completed document? Complete, or just done? No document is	25	8
quite complete until it has left you and passed to the next step.	38	13
There are desirable things that must happen to a document before	13	17
you surrender it. It must be read carefully, first of all, for	26	22
meaning to find words that look right but aren't. Read word for	39	26
word.	40	26
Check all figures and exact data, like a date or time, with your	13	31
principal copy. Make sure format details are right. Only then,	26	35
print or remove the work and scrutinize to see how it might look	39	39
to a recipient.	42	40

1' | 1 | 2 | 3 | 4 | 5 | 6 | 7 | 8 | 9 | 10 | 11 | 12 | 13 |
3' | 1 | 2 | 3 | 4 |

17e Improve Keystroking

first finger

17 buy them gray vent guy brunt buy brunch much give huge vying

18 Hagen, after her July triumph at tennis, may try volleyball.

19 Verna urges us to buy yet another of her beautiful rag rugs.

second finger

20 keen idea; kick it back; ice breaker; decide the issue; cite

21 Did Dick ask Cecelia, his sister, if she decided to like me?

22 Suddenly, Micki's bike skidded on the Cedar Street ice rink.

third/fourth finger

23 low slow lax solo wax zip zap quips quiz zipper prior icicle

24 Paula has always allowed us to relax at La Paz and at Quito.

25 Please ask Zale to explain who explores most aquatic slopes.

17f Timed Writing

Take a 2' timing on all the paragraphs. Repeat the timing. Use wordwrap.

	gwam	2'	3'

Many experts believe stress affects the mind as well as the body. However, they are not quite sure just how much damage can be caused. This may be because people deal with stress in several different ways. Some learn to either shrug it off or else put little thought to it.

Coping with stress is difficult but if one is willing to make an effort, it can be handled easily. One way to deal with stress is having a good diet as well as regular exercise. Another way is to become involved with enjoyable activities such as writing, painting, or running. Last, but certainly not least, have a positive thought process, a great zest for life, and a big cheerful smile.

gwam 2'|3':
6|4
11|8
17|12
23|16
27|19
34|23
39|27
46|31
52|35
58|39
64|43
67|45

17g Enrichment

1. From the Skill Building tab, choose Technique Builder; Drill 2.
2. Key Drill 2 from page 38. Key each line once, striving for good acuracy.
3. The results will be listed on the Skill Building Report.
4. Log out of *KPDO*.

Skill Building *Technique Builder*

Select the Skill Building tab from the Main menu and then Technique Builder. Select the drill and follow the directions in the book.

DRILL 8

Opposite Hand Reaches

Key each line once and DS between groups of lines. Key at a controlled rate; concentrate on the reaches.

i/e
1 ik is fit it sit laid site like insist still wise coil light
2 ed he ear the fed egg led elf lake jade heat feet hear where
3 lie kite item five aide either quite linear imagine brighter
4 Imagine the aide eating the pears before the grieving tiger.

w/o
5 ws we way was few went wit law with weed were week gnaw when
6 ol on go hot old lot joy odd comb open tool upon money union
7 bow owl word wood worm worse tower brown toward wrote weapon
8 The workers lowered the brown swords toward the wood weapon.

DRILL 9

Proofreaders' Marks

Key each line once and DS after each sentence. Correct the sentence as edited, making all handwritten corrections. Do not key the numbers.

≡ Capitalize
/ Change letter
⌒ Close up space
ℐ Delete
∧ Insert
ℓc Lowercase
Space
ᴎ Transpose

1. When a writer create the preliminary version of a document, they are concentrating on conveying the intended ideas.
2. This ver sion of a preliminary document is called a rough draft.
3. After the draft is created the Writer edits/refines the copy.
4. Sometimes proofreader's marks are used to edit the draft.
5. The changes will them be make to the original. editing
6. After the changes have been made, then the Writer reads the copy again.
7. Edit ing and proofreading requires alot of time and effort.
8. An attitute of excellance is required to produce error free message.

DRILL 10

Proofreading

Compare your sentences in Drill 9 with Drill 10. How did you do? Now key the paragraph for fluency. Concentrate on keying as accurately as possible.

When a writer creates the preliminary version of a document, he or she is concentrating on conveying ideas. This preliminary version is called a rough draft. After the draft is created, the writer edits or refines the copy. Proofreaders' marks are used to edit the rough draft. The editing changes will be made to the original. Then the writer reads the copy again. Editing requires a lot of time and effort. An attitude of excellence is required to produce an error-free message.

Lesson 18 3 and 6

Warmup *Lesson 18a Warmup*

New Keys

18b   3 and 6

3 Reach *up* with *left second* finger.

6 Reach *up* with *right first* finger.

Note: Ergonomic keyboard users will use *left first* finger to key 6.

3

1 3 3d d3 3 3; had 3 days; did 3 dives; led 3 dogs; add 3 dips
2 we 3 ride 3 cars; take 33 dials; read 3 copies; save 33 days
3 On July 3, 33 lights lit 33 stands holding 33 prize winners.

6

4 6 6j 6j 6 6; 6 jays; 6 jams; 6 jigs; 6 jibs; 6 jots; 6 jokes
5 only 6 high; on 66 units; reach 66 numbers; 6 yams or 6 jams
6 On May 6, Car 66 delivered 66 tons of No. 6 shale to Pier 6.

18c   All Figures Learned

7 At 6 p.m., Channel 3 reported the August 6 score was 6 to 3.
8 Jean, do Items 28 and 6; Mika, 59 and 10; Kyle, 3, 4, and 7.
9 Cars 56 and 34 used Aisle 9; Cars 2 and 87 can use Aisle 10.

18d   Textbook Keying

Key each line once.

word response: *think* and *key* words

10 he el id is go us it an me of he of to if ah or bye do so am
11 Did she enamel emblems on a big panel for the downtown sign?

stroke response: *think* and *key* each stroke

12 kin are hip read lymph was pop saw ink art oil gas up as mop
13 Barbara started the union wage earners tax in Texas in July.

combination response: *vary speed but maintain rhythm*

14 upon than eve lion when burley with they only them loin were
15 It was the opinion of my neighbor that we may work as usual.

25e Figure Check

In the Word Processor, key two 3' writings at a controlled rate. Save the timings as xx-25e-t1 and xx-25e-t2. Use wordwrap.

Goal: 3', 14–16 gwam.

Do people read the stock market pages in the news? Yes;   4
at approximately 9 or 10 a.m. each morning, I know lots of   8
excited people who do that. Some people still like to have the 12
paper delivered to their home each morning. Others like the 16
convenience of reading the news on their computer or their 20
cell phone. Nevertheless, we can't wait to obtain the first 24
stock report each day. 26

Some people take the stock market very seriously. They 30
watch their stocks carefully and note the rise and fall of 34
each stock. Most investors like to be able to "buy at 52 and 38
sell at 60." Some would like to receive a dividend of 7 or 8 42
percent on their stocks. Regardless, each morning we zip 45
immediately to the stock report to see how the market is 49
doing. When the stock is down, we quickly purchase more shares 53
and keep them until they increase in value. The stock market 58
is an important and vital part of our life. 60

3' | 1 | 2 | 3 | 4 |

Communication

25f Edit Copy

1. In the Word Processor, key your name, class, and date at the left margin.
2. Key the paragraphs and make the corrections marked with proofreaders' marks. Use the BACK-SPACE key to correct errors.
3. Check number expressions.
4. Save as xx-25f.

Last week the healthy heart foundation released the findings of a study that showed exercise diet and if individuals don't smoke are the major controllable factors that led to a healthy heart. Factors such as heredity can not be controlled. The study included 25 to 65 year old males as well as females. women especially benefited from

The study also showed that just taking a walk benefits our health. Those who walked an average of 2 to 3 hours a week were more then 30 percent less likely to have problems than those who did no exercise.

25g Proofread and Edit

Learn More:

www.cengagebrain.com

1. In the Word Processor, open xx-24Rd.
2. Turn to page 70 and proofread your document with Writing 11.
3. Make corrections as needed. Save as xx-25g. Print.

18e Improve Keystroking

long reaches

16 ce cede cedar wreck nu nu nut punt nuisance my my amy mystic
17 ny ny any many company mu mu mull lumber mulch br br furbish
18 Cecil received a large brown umbrella from Bunny and Hunter.

number review

19 set 0; push 4; Car 00; score 44; jot 04; age 40; Billet 4004
20 April 5; lock 5; set 66; fill 55; hit 65; pick 56; adds 5665
21 Her grades are 93, 87, and 100; his included 82, 96, and 54.

18f Timed Writing

Key two 3' writings. Use wordwrap.

Jim West/Alamy

gwam 3'

I am something quite precious. Though millions of people	4
in other countries might not have me, you likely do. I am very	8
powerful. I choose the new president every four years. I	12
decide if a tax should be levied or repealed. I even decide	16
questions of war and peace. I was acquired with great expense;	20
however, I am free to all citizens. But sadly enough, I am	24
often ignored; or, still worse, I am just taken for granted. I	28
can be lost, and in certain circumstances I can even be taken	33
away. What am I? I am your right to vote. Don't take me	36
lightly. Exercise your right to vote at every election;	40
consider it an opportunity and a privilege.	43

3' | 1 | 2 | 3 | 4 |

Communication

18g Composition

📄 Word Processor

1. Go to the Word Processor. Compose two paragraphs, each having about three sentences, in which you introduce yourself to your instructor. Use proper grammatical structure. Disregard keying errors at this time.

2. Save the document as *xx-profile*; replace *xx* with your initials. You will edit this document later.

Lesson 25 Assessment

Skill Building

25b Improve Keystroking

n/y
1 deny many canny tiny nymph puny any puny zany penny pony yen
2 Jenny Nyles saw many, many tiny nymphs flying near her pony.

b/r
3 bran barb brim curb brat garb bray verb brag garb bribe herb
4 Barb Barber can bring a bit of bran and herbs for her bread.

c/e
5 cede neck nice deck dice heck rice peck vice erect mice echo
6 Can Cedric erect a decent cedar deck? He erects nice condos.

n/u
7 nun gnu bun nut pun numb sun nude tuna nub fun null unit gun
8 Eunice had enough ground nuts at lunch; Uncle Launce is fun.

25c Textbook Keying

Key each line once.

9 is if he do rub ant go and am pan do rut us aid ox ape by is
10 it is|an end|it may|to pay|and so|aid us|he got|or own|to go
11 Did the girl make the ornament with fur, duck down, or hair?

12 us owl rug box bob to man so bit or big pen of jay me age it
13 it|it is|time to go|show them how|plan to go|one of the aims
14 It is a shame they use the autobus for a visit to the field.

25d Timed Writing

Key two 3' writings. Strive for accuracy. Use wordwrap.

Goal: 3', 19–27 *gwam*.

> **Build confidence—trust your reach instincts.**

gwam 3'

  The term career can mean many different things to   4
different people. As you know, a career is more than just an   8
occupation. It includes the jobs an individual has over time.   12
It also involves how the work life affects the other parts of   16
our life. There are as many types of careers as there are   20
people.   20

  Almost every person has a career of some kind. A career   24
can help us attain unique goals, such as having a stable   28
livelihood or a rewarding vocation. The kind of career you   32
have will affect your life in many ways. For example, it can   36
determine where you live, the money you make, and how you feel   40
about yourself. A good choice can thus help you realize the   44
life you want.   45

3' | 1 | 2 | 3 | 4 |

Lesson 18R Review

Skill Building

18Rb Textbook Keying

Key each line once; work for fluency.

1 Jake may pay the sixty men for eighty bushels of blue forks.
2 We used software versions 1.01, 2.6, 7.2, 8.3, 8.5, and 9.4.
3 The big box by the lake held fish, duck, apricot, and a map.
4 Adding 123 and 345 and 567 and 80 and 62 and 5 totals 1,182.
5 Lana and Jay and Ken paid to sit by the lake to fish at six.
6 We can see you at 6:30, 7:30, 8:45, 9:00, or 12:15 tomorrow.

18Rc Timed Writing

Key a 3' timing on all paragraphs. Repeat.

gwam 3'

You want to be known as a person of good character. If 4
someone says that you have character, it usually means that 8
you are honest, have integrity, and are reliable and 12
responsible. On the other hand, if you lie, cheat, or steal, 16
or are lazy, you will be known as a person with poor 19
character. If others say that you are quite a character, it 23
usually means that you have good character. 26

You will be judged by your actions and expressions. What 30
you say and do to others affects how others will respond to 34
you. You need to be considerate of others and conscientious in 38
your work. Others will respect and trust you and want you 42
involved in their activities. 44

LA **ALL LETTERS**

3' | 1 | 2 | 3 | 4 |

Communication

18Rd Number Expression

1. From the Reference tab, click Communication Skills; select Number Expression.
2. Complete the pretest; click Report to review your results.

18Re Enrichment

1. In the Word Processor, take a 30" timing on the first line; repeat the line as many times as possible.
2. Take a 30" timing on the second line. Try to maintain the same speed as the first line.

7 Come work with us on this new job next month.
8 Jo will be 44 years 2 months and 24 days old.
9 I see you need some help with the new assignments.
10 I will be 44 years 2 months and 24 days old today.
11 Sixteen of us can come and help you today and tomorrow.
12 Order 99 cookies; at least have 33 sugar and 39 ginger.
13 Tell us how you want the work done; we will finish it today.
14 We must deliver order 6688 for 88 chairs and 66 tables by 6.

Lesson 24R Review

Skill Building

Warmup *Lesson 24Ra Warmup*

24Rb Textbook Keying

Key each line once; work for fluency.

1 E-mail invoice #397 to gmeathe@skd.org; the $7 will be paid.
2 Jane and Ken may go to town to handle the pale and sick dog.
3 The answers to pop quiz #12 are: (1) a, (2) c, (3) b, (4) c.
4 Uncle Jeff rented a burgundy minivan for three days a month.
5 Check #42 was sent on 6/15 for the amount of $89 as payment.
6 Zale played amazing pop jazz on a saxophone and a xylophone.
7 L & D Bank pays 7% interest on savings accounts, 10% on CDs.

24Rc Timed Writing

1. Key a 1' timing on each paragraph; work to increase speed.
2. Key a 3' timing on all paragraphs.

	gwam	1'	3'
Do you find yourself forgetting the names of people that		12	4
you have known for quite some time? Did you put something down		25	8
and a few minutes later were not able to find it again? Memory		37	12
lapses like these are normal, and there are things you can do		50	17
to prevent them from happening as often. Just a few simple		62	21
lifestyle changes can easily help improve your emory.		72	24
Everyone can take steps to better their memory; it will		12	28
take both time and practice. It is important to get enough		24	32
sleep and to eat properly. Exercise both the mind and the		36	36
body. Read, write, and do puzzles each day to help develop		47	44
your memory. Make time for family and friends and have a good		60	48
time with them.		63	49

```
1' |  1  |  2  |  3  |  4  |  5  |  6  |  7  |  8  |  9  |  10  |  11  |  12  |
3' |        1        |         2         |         3         |         4         |
```

24Rd Enrichment

Word Processor

1. Key the paragraphs in the Word Processor, making revisions as you key.
2. Key your name and 24Rd below the paragraph.
3. Save as *xx-24Rd*.

Any one who expects someday to find an excellent job should learn
[#] [great] [begin now to] [final]

the value of accuracy. To be worth any thing, completed work must [be]
correct, [Of course,] [human]
accurate, without any question. Naturally we realize that the aspect of the
[but] [understand]

work equation raises/always the chance of errors; we should know that
errors
those same mistakes can be found and fixed. Every job completed should
[sp] [true pride] [exemplary]

carry at least 1 stamp; the stamp of approval in work that is outstanding.

Lesson 19 $ and – (hyphen), Number Expression

19b Learn $ and -

$ Shift; then reach *up* with *left first* finger.

- (hyphen) Reach *up* with *right fourth* finger.

- = **hyphen**
-- = **dash**
Do not space before or after a hyphen or a dash.

$

1 $ $f f$ $ $; if $4; half $4; off $4; of $4; $4 fur; $4 flats
2 for $8; cost $9; log $3; grab $10; give Rolf $2; give Viv $4
3 Since she paid $45 for the item priced at $54, she saved $9.

- (hyphen)

4 - -; ;- - - -; up-to-date; co-op; father-in-law; four-square
5 pop-up foul; big-time job; snap-on bit; one- or two-hour ski
6 You need 6 signatures--half of the members--on the petition.

19c All Symbols Learned

7 I paid $10 for the low-cost disk; high-priced ones cost $40.
8 Le-An spent $20 for travel, $95 for books, and $38 for food.
9 Mr. Loft-Smit sold his boat for $467; he bought it for $176.

Skill Building

19d Improve Keystroking

10 Edie discreetly decided to deduct expenses in making a deal.
11 Working women wear warm wool sweaters when weather dictates.
12 We heard very rude remarks regarding her recent termination.
13 Daily sudden mishaps destroyed several dozens of sand dunes.
14 Beverley voted by giving a bold beverage to every brave boy.

Skill Building

24c Improve Keystroking

double letters
13 feel pass mill good miss seem moons cliffs pools green spell
14 Assets are being offered in a stuffy room to two associates.

balanced hand
15 is if of to it go do to is do so if to the to sign it vie to
16 Pamela or Jen may also go to town with Blanche if she works.

24d Timed Writing

Take two 3' timings.
Use wordwrap.

	gwam 3'
Why do we resist change so much? Do you think perhaps it	4
is because it requires more time and effort learning new	8
things and making difficult decisions? Is it also because we	12
are set in our ways, afraid to take chances and dislike being	16
told what to do? Besides, what is the point of trying to	20
improve something that works just fine?	22
We know change can and does extend new areas of	26
enjoyment, areas we might never have known existed. If we stay	30
away from all change, we could curtail our quality of life.	34
People who are open to change are more zealous and more	38
productive than those who aren't. They are also better at	42
coping with the hardships and challenges that life often	46
brings.	46

3' | 1 | 2 | 3 | 4 |

Communication

24e Composition

Word Processor

1. In the Word Processor, open the file *xx-profile* that you created in Lesson 18.
2. Position the insertion point at the end of the last paragraph. Tap ENTER twice.
3. Key an additional paragraph that begins with the following sentence:
   Thank you for allowing me to introduce myself.
4. Finish the paragraph by adding two or more sentences that describe your progress and satisfaction with keyboarding.
5. Correct any mistakes you have made. Click Save to resave the document. Print.
6. Mark any mistakes you missed with proofreaders' marks. Revise the document and save. Submit to your instructor.

24f Edit Copy

1. In the Word Processor, key your name, class, and date at the left margin on separate lines.
2. Key each line, making the corrections marked with proofreaders' marks.
3. Proofread and correct errors using the BACKSPACE key.
4. Save as *xx-24f*.

17 Ask Group 1 to read Chater 6 of Book 11 (Shelf 19, Room 5).

18 All 6 of us live at One Bay road, not at 126-56th Street.

19 AT 9 a.m. the owners decided to close form 12 noon to 1 p.m.

20 Ms. Vik leaves June 9; she returns the 14 or 15 of July.

21 The 16 percent discount saves $115. A stamp costs 44 cents.

22 Elin gave $300,000,000; our gift was only 75 cents.

19e Textbook Keying

1. Key each line once.
2. When keying easy words and phrases:
   - Think and key words and phrases rather than letter by letter.
   - Make the space part of the word.

easy words

15 am it go bus dye jam irk six sod tic yam ugh spa vow aid dug
16 he or by air big elf dog end fit and lay sue toe wit own got
17 six foe pen firm also body auto form down city kept make fog

easy phrases

18 it is│if the│and also│to me│the end│to us│if it│it is│to the
19 if it is│to the end│do you wish│to go to│for the end│to make
20 lay down│he or she│make me│by air│end of│by me│kept it│of me

easy sentences

21 Did the chap work to mend the torn right half of the ensign?
22 Blame me for their penchant for the antique chair and panel.
23 She bid by proxy for eighty bushels of a corn and rye blend.

19f Textbook Keying

1. Review the Number Expression Guidelines 1–4 in the Reference Guide. Then key sentences 24–29.
2. Key lines 30–35. Decide whether the circled numbers should be keyed as figures or as words and make needed changes.

> **Key numbers without watching your fingers.**

24 **Six** or **seven** older players were cut from the **37**-member team.
25 I have **2** of **14** coins I need to start my set. Christen has **9**.
26 Of **nine 24**-ton engines ordered, we shipped **six** last Tuesday.
27 Shelly has read just **one-half** of about **forty-five** documents.
28 The **six** boys sent well over **two hundred** printed invitations.
29 **One** or **two** of us will be on duty from **two** until **six** o'clock.

30 Jan will come by at ④ o'clock to pick up the ③ girls.
31 Lauren and Paul invited ②⓪⓪ guests to the reception.
32 We have ③ more days to finish ②/③ of the plan.
33 Tish sent ⑦ ㉔-pound boxes and ⑩ ③-ounce envelopes.
34 I deposited ⑮ quarters, ⑩ dimes, and ④ nickels in the ATM.
35 A quorum was established; ⑦ of the ⑫ members voted.

19g Enrichment

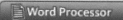

1. From the Timed Writings tab, choose Writing 2.
2. Set the timing length for 1'.
3. Locate Writing 2 on page 40 and key it twice. Strive to increase speed by 2 gwam the second time.
4. Log out of *KPDO*.

Lesson 24 Other Symbols

 **Warmup** *Lesson 24a Warmup*

New Keys

24b Textbook Keying

@   *   +   =

@	at
*	asterisk
+	plus sign (use a hyphen for minus and x for "times")
=	equals

Be confident—watch the copy, not the hands.

@ shift; reach *up* with *left third* finger to @

1 @ @s s@ a a; 24 @ .15; 22 @ .35; sold 2 @ .87; were 12 @ .95

2 You may contact Calvin @: CEP@rpx.com or fax @ 602.555.0101.

3 E-mail Al ajj@crewl.com and Matt mrw10@scxs.com by 9:30 p.m.

* shift; reach *up* with *right second* finger to *

4 * *k k8* * *; aurelis*; May 7*; both sides*; 250 km.**; aka*

5 Note each *; one * refers to page 29; ** refers to page 307.

6 Use *.* to search for files; the * looks for all characters.

+ shift; reach *up* with *right fourth* finger to +

7 + ;+ +; + + +; 2 + 2; A+ or B+; 70+ F. degrees; +xy over +y;

8 The question was 8 + 7 + 51; it should have been 8 + 7 + 15.

9 My grades on the tests and final exam are B+, C+, B+, and A.

= reach *up* with *right fourth* finger to =

10 = =; = = =; = 4; If 14x = 28, x = 2; if 8x = 16, then x = 2.

11 Change this solution (where it says "= by") to = bx or = BX.

12 Key the formula =(a2+b2)*d5/4 in the formula bar; tap Enter.

Lesson 20 # and /

New Keys

20b   Learn # and /

Shift; then reach *up* with *left second* finger.

/ Reach *down* with *right fourth* finger.

> **#** = number sign, pounds
> **/** = diagonal, slash

#

1 # #e e# # # #; had #3 dial; did #3 drop; set #3 down; Bid #3

2 leave #82; sold #20; Lyric #16; bale #34; load #53; Optic #7

3 Notice #333 says to load Car #33 with 33# of #3 grade shale.

/

4 / /; ;/ / / /; 1/2; 1/3; Mr./Mrs.; 1/4/12; 22 11/12; and/or;

5 to/from; /s/ William Smit; 2/10, n/30; his/her towels; 6 1/2

6 The numerals 1 5/8, 3 1/4, and 60 7/9 are "mixed fractions."

20c   All Symbols Learned

7 Invoice #737 cites 15 2/3# of rye was shipped C.O.D. 4/6/14.

8 B-O-A Company's Check #50/5 for $87 paid for 15# of #3 wire.

9 Our Co-op List #20 states $40 for 16 1/2 crates of tomatoes.

Skill Building

20d   Build Skill

Strive to maintain your speed on the second line in the pair.

10 She did the key work at the height of the problem.

11 Form #726 is the title to the island; she owns it.

12 The rock is a form of fuel; he did enrich it with coal.

13 The corn-and-turkey dish is a blend of turkey and corn.

14 It is right to work to end the social problems of the world.

15 If I sign it on 3/19, the form can aid us to pay the 40 men.

16 Profit problems at the firm may cause it to take many risks.

17 Dale discovered that Invoice #238 for $128.83 is dated 8/15.

23e Improve Keystroking

double letters

17 Do Bennett was puzzled by drivers exceeding the speed limit.

18 Bill needs the office address; he will cut the grass at ten.

19 Todd saw the green car veer off the street near a tall tree.

figures and symbols

20 Invoice #84 for $672.90, plus $4.38 tax, was due February 3.

21 Do read Section 4, pages 60–74 and Section 9, pages 198–225.

22 Enter as follows: (a) name, (b) address, and (c) cell phone.

23f Timed Writing

Take two 3' timings. Use wordwrap.

gwam 3'

Is how you judge my work important? Does your honest   4
opinion or feedback really matter? It does, of course; I hope   8
you appreciate the effort and recognize some basic merit in   12
it. We all expect to get credit for the hard work we put forth   16
and the good work we conclude. After all, we are all working   20
together to accomplish the goals of the company.   23

As a human being, I want approval for the ideas   27
presented, things written, and tasks completed. I always look   31
forward to your evaluations so I can learn more and continue   35
to grow. My work does not define me, but it shows my abilities   39
and skills. Through my work, I am my very own unique self.   43

3' | 1 | 2 | 3 | 4 |

Communication

23g Edit Text

Word Processor

1. In the Word Processor, key your name, class, and **23g** at the left margin. Then key lines 23–28, making the revisions as you key. Use the BACKSPACE key to correct errors.

2. Proofread and correct errors.

3. Save as xx-23g.

Symbol	Meaning	Symbol	Meaning
———	Italic	◯ sp	Spell out
~~	Bold	¶	Paragraph
Cap or ═══	Capitalize	#	Add horizontal space
∧	Insert	/ or lc	Lowercase
⸮	Delete	‿	Close up space
⌐	Move to left	～	Transpose
⌐_	Move to right	stet	Leave as originally written

23 We miss 50% in life's rewards by refusing to new try things.

24 do it now--today--then tomorrow's load will be 100%% lighter.

25 Satisfying work- whether it pays $40 or $400-is the pay off.

26 Avoid mistakes: confusing a #3 has cost thousands.

27 Pleased most with a first-rate job is the person who did it.

28 My wife and/or me mother will except the certificate for me.

20e Textbook Keying

Key each line once. Notice the difference in the rhythm of your keying.

one hand
18 lip ere him bat lion date pink face pump rear only brag fact
19 at my; oh no; add debt; extra milk; union agreed; act faster

balanced hand
20 so it is | now is the | do so when | sign the forms | is it downtown
21 He may wish to go to town with Pamela to sign the amendment.

combination
22 was for | in the case of | they were | to down | pink bowls | wet rugs
23 They were to be down in the fastest sleigh if you are right.

20f Timed Writing

1. Key a 1' timing on each paragraph; work to increase speed.
2. Key a 3' timing on all paragraphs.

LA ALL LETTERS

	gwam	1'	3'
Most people want to be socially acceptable. In some		11	4
cases, the need for attention can lead to difficulties. Some		23	8
of us think that the best way to get attention is to try a new		36	12
style, or to look quixotic, or to be different somehow.		47	16
Perhaps we are looking for nothing much more than acceptance		59	20
from others of ourselves just the way we now are.		68	23
There is no question about it; we all want to look our		12	27
best to impress other people. How this is achieved may mean		24	31
that we try something new, or perform things differently.		35	34
Regardless, our basic objective is to continue to build		46	38
character with zeal from our raw materials, you and me.		57	42

1' | 1 | 2 | 3 | 4 | 5 | 6 | 7 | 8 | 9 | 10 | 11 | 12 |
3' | 1 | 2 | 3 | 4 |

Communication

20g Number Expression

Word Processor

1. Review Number Expression in the Reference Guide.
2. In the Word Processor, key sentences 24–27 below. Do not use bold.
3. Key sentences 28 and 29, applying the rules correctly.

24 Ask **Group 2** to read **Chapter 7** of **Book 11** (**Shelf 19, Room 5**).
25 All **six** of us live at **One Bay Lane**, not at **142--59th Street**.
26 At **8 a.m.** the owners decided to close from **12 noon** to **1 p.m.**
27 Ms. Han leaves **June 3**; she returns the **14th or 15th of July**.
28 The 16 percent discount saves $123.50. The tax was 75 cents.
29 Jim poured 3 six-liter jars of oil into the 9 gallon barrel.

Lesson 23 & and : (colon), Proofreaders' Marks

New Keys

23b & and : (Colon)

& Shift; then reach *up* with *right first* finger.

: (colon) Left shift; then tap key with *right fourth* finger.

& = ampersand: The ampersand is used only as part of company names.

Colon: Space once after a colon except when used within a number for time.

& (ampersand)

1 & &j j& & & &; J & J; Haraj & Jay; Moroj & Jax; Torj & Jones
2 Nehru & Unger; Mumm & Just; Mann & Hart; Arch & Jones; M & J
3 Rhye & Knox represent us; Steb & Doy, Firm A; R & J, Firm B.

: (colon)

4 : :; ;: : : :; as: for example: notice: Dear Sir: Gentlemen:
5 In stock: 10:30; 7:45; Age: Address: Read: Cell: Attachment:
6 Space once after a colon, thus: Telephone: Home Address: To:

23c All Symbols Learned

7 Consider these companies: J & R, Brand & Kay, Upper & Davis.
8 Memo #88-829 reads as follows: "Deduct 15% of $300, or $45."
9 Bill 32(5)--it got here quite late--from M & N was paid 7/3.

Skill Building

23d Textbook Keying

Key each line once.

10 *Jane may work with an auditing firm if she is paid to do so.*
11 *Pam and eight girls may go to the lake to work with the dog.*
12 *Clancy and Claudia did all the work to fix the sign problem.*
13 *Did Lea visit the Orlando land of enchantment or a neighbor?*
14 *Ana and Blanche made a map for a neighbor to go to the city.*
15 *Sidney may go to the lake to fish with worms from the docks.*
16 *Did the firm or the neighbors own the auto with the problem?*

Lesson 21 % and !

Warmup *Lesson 21a Warmup*

New Keys

21b % and !

% Shift; then reach *up* with *left first* finger.

⭐ **TIP**

- Do not space between a figure and the % or $ sign.
- Do not space before or after the dash.

% = percent sign:
Use % with business forms or where space is restricted; otherwise use the word "percent."

Space once after the exclamation point!

© Cengage Learning

%

1 % %f f% % %; off 5%; if 5%; of 5% fund; half 5%; taxes of 5%

2 7% rent; 3% tariff; 9% F.O.B.; 15% greater; 28% base; up 46%

3 Give discounts of 5% on rods, 50% on lures, and 75% on line.

! reach up with the left 4th finger

4 ! !a a! ! ! !; Eureka! Ha! No! Pull 10! Extra! America! Yea!

5 Attention! Now! Ready! On your mark! Get set! Go! Good show!

6 We need it now, not next week! I am sure to lose 50% or $19.

21c All Symbols Learned

7 The ad offers a 10% discount, but this notice says 15% less!

8 He got the job! With Loehman's Supermarket! Please call Mom!

9 Bill #92-44 arrived very late from Zyclone; it was paid 7/4.

21d Improve Keystroking

all symbols

10 As of 6/28, Jeri owes $31 for dinner and $27 for cab fare.

11 Invoice #20--it was dated 3/4--billed $17 less 15% discount.

12 He deducted 2% instead of 6%, a clear saving of 6% vs. 7%.

combination response

13 Look at my dismal grade in English; but I guess I earned it.

14 Kris started to blend a cocoa beverage for a shaken cowhand.

15 Jan may make a big profit if she owns the title to the land.

22e Timed Writing

1. Take two 3' timings on both paragraphs.
2. End the lesson.
3. Go to the Word Processor and complete 22f.

It is our obligation to preserve the planet and hand it   4
down to our children and grandchildren in a better condition   8
than when we first found it. We must take extra steps just to   12
make the quality of living better. Unless we change our ways   16
and stop damaging the environment, the world will not be a   20
good place to live.   22

To help save our ozone layer, we should not use any   25
products that may have harmful gas in them. There are many   29
simple and easy ways to clean the air such as planting more   33
trees and reusing materials. Also as important is the proper   37
disposal of our garbage in order to stop our water from   41
getting more and more polluted.   43

3' | 1 | 2 | 3 | 4 |

22f Backspace Key

Word Processor

1. Key sentences 16–21 in the Word Processor; use the BACKSPACE key to correct errors.
2. Key the numbers correctly in sentences 22–26. Refer to the Number Expression section in the Reference Guide.
3. Proofread and correct errors.
4. Save as *xx-22f* (your initials–22f). Print and close the document.

Use the Backspace key effectively.

16 You should be interested in the special items on sale today.
17 If she is going with us, why don't we plan to leave now?
18 Do you desire to continue working on the memo in the future?
19 Did the firm or their neighbors own the autos with problems?
20 Juni, Vec, and Zeb had perfect grades on weekly query exams.
21 Jewel quickly explained to me the big fire hazards involved.

22 All 7 contracts must be signed before 3 o'clock p.m.
23 Purchase 2 16-gigabyte USB flash drives; they are on sale.
24 Jim poured 3 six-liter jars of oil into the 9 gallon barrel.
25 My last computer project is approximately 1/2 complete.
26 The 16 percent discount saves $123.50. The tax was 75 cents.

Communication

22g Proofreading

1. From the Reference tab, click Communication Skills; select Proofreading.
2. Complete the pretest; click Report to review your results. Review the rules and complete the exercises and posttest.

21e Textbook Keying

Key each line once.

1st finger

16 by bar get fun van for inn art from gray hymn July true verb

17 brag human bring unfold hominy mighty report verify puny joy

18 You are brave to try bringing home the van in the bad storm.

2nd finger

19 ace ink did cad keyed deep seed kind Dick died kink like kid

20 cease decease decades kick secret check decide kidney evaded

21 Dedre likes the idea of ending dinner with cake for dessert.

3rd finger

22 oil sow six vex wax axe low old lox pool west loss wool slow

23 swallow swamp saw sew wood sax sexes loom stew excess school

24 Wes waxes floors and washes windows at low costs to schools.

4th finger

25 zap zip craze pop pup pan daze quote queen quiz pizza puzzle

26 zoo graze zipper panzer zebra quip partizan patronize appear

27 Czar Zane appears to be dazzled by the apple pizza and jazz.

21f Timed Writing

1. Key a 1' timing on each paragraph.
2. Key a 3' timing on both paragraphs.

	gwam	1'	3'
Teams are the basic unit of performance for a firm. They		12	4
are not the solution to all the problems and needs of the		24	8
organization. However, they can perform at a higher rate		35	12
compared to other groups. Their support has great impact on		47	16
changes that are crucial to a firm.		54	18
Teams are not established just by joining people together		13	22
in a group. Team members should have a clear purpose and they		25	26
should also work with each other to reach a common goal. In		37	30
order to make a quality working plan, the team must maximize		49	38
their time and their abilities. They need to learn how to help		62	39
one another and make an effort to coordinate the tasks.		73	42

```
1' |  1  |  2  |  3  |  4  |  5  |  6  |  7  |  8  |  9  |  10 |  11 |  12 |
3' |        1        |        2        |        3        |        4        |
```

21g Enrichment

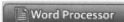

Take two 1' writings; the last number you key is your approximate *gwam*.

Reach for numbers with a minimum of hand movement.

1 and 2 and 3 and 4 and 5 and 6 and 7 and 8 and 9 and 10 and 11 and 12 and 13 and 14 and 15 and 16 and 17 and 18 and 19 and 20 and 21 and 22 and 23 and 24 and 25 and 26 and 27 and

Lesson 22 (and) and Backspace Key

Warmup *Lesson 22a Warmup*

New Keys

22b (and)

(Shift; then reach *up* with the *right third* finger.

) Shift; then reach *up* with the *right fourth* finger.

> **( ) = parentheses**
> Parentheses indicate off-hand, aside, or explanatory messages.

1 ((l l((; (; Reach from l for the left parenthesis; as, ((.

2)); ;))); Reach from ; for the right parenthesis; as,)).

( )

3 Learn to use parentheses (plural) or parenthesis (singular).

4 The red (No. 34) and blue (No. 78) cars both won here (Rio).

5 We (Galen and I) dined (bagels) in our penthouse (the dorm).

22c All Symbols Learned

6 The jacket was $35 (thirty-five dollars)--the tie was extra.

7 Starting 10/29, you can sell Model #49 at a discount of 25%.

8 My size 8 1/2 shoe--a blue pump--was soiled (but not badly).

Skill Building

22d Textbook Keying

Key each line once.

> *Build confidence—trust yourself to make the correct reach.*

9 Jana has one hard-to-get copy of her hot-off-the-press book.

10 An invoice said that "We give discounts of 10%, 5%, and 3%."

11 The company paid bill 8/07 on 5/2/14 and bill 4/9 on 3/6/14.

12 The catalog lists as out of stock Items #230, #710, and #13.

13 Ellyn had $8; Sean, $9; and Cal, $7. The cash total was $24.

14 A representative from the 16th District (Tom Law) will come.

15 The oldest family member (May Gray) will attend the reunion.

Reference Guide

Windows 8

START WINDOWS 8

Windows 8 is an operating system software released by Microsoft. The operating system software controls the operations of the computer and works with the application software. *Windows 8* works with *Word* in opening, printing, deleting, and saving files. It also allows you to work with photos, play music and videos, and access the Internet.

When you turn on your computer, the *Windows 8* Lock screen displays. Press any key to display the *Windows 8* Sign-in screen. Key your password and press ENTER to display the *Windows 8* Start Screen.

Windows 8 Lock screen

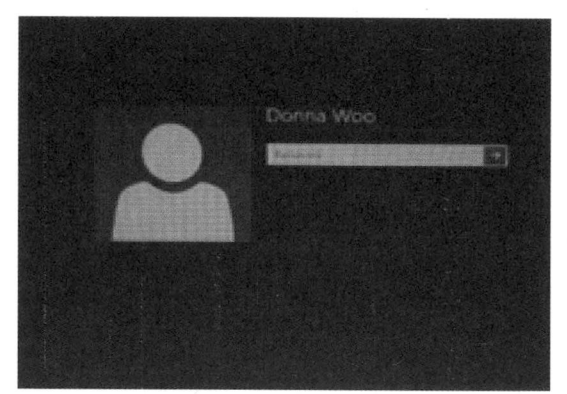

Windows 8 Sign-in screen

WINDOWS 8 START SCREEN

The *Windows 8* Start screen contains tiles that represent an application or a *Windows 8* feature; click the tile to start the application. Some tiles are live in that they show updated information, such as the Weather, News, and Finance tiles. If you do not see the tile for the application that you wish to launch, scroll to the right to view more apps, or right-click an empty spot on the Start screen and click the **All apps** button in the lower-right. The Desktop tile, in the lower-left, provides access to the *Windows 8* desktop.

To display the Start screen from any location, tap the Windows key (⊞) or move the mouse to the lower-left corner of the screen to display the Start icon and click on it.

Desktop Tile ⟶

WINDOWS 8 DESKTOP

The *Windows 8* desktop displays when you click the Desktop tile on the *Windows 8* Start screen. To display the desktop from any location, press ⊞ + D. Refer to the illustration below to familiarize yourself with the basic screen elements.

- ■ *Taskbar* ❶. The taskbar displays across the bottom of the window. Use the mouse to point to each item in the taskbar. Look for the ScreenTip that displays identifying each element.

  - • *Program and file buttons.* Buttons display for the programs that are open or pinned to the taskbar and allow you to switch between them easily. The *Internet Explorer* ❷ icon is displayed to provide quick access to the Internet. The *File Explorer* ❸ icon provides quick access to your files.

  - • *Notification area* ❹. The notification area provides helpful information, such as the date and time and the status of the computer. When you plug in a USB drive, *Windows* displays an icon in the notification area letting you know that the hardware is connected.

- ■ *Icons and Shortcuts* ❺. Icons, small pictures representing certain items, may be displayed on the desktop. The Recycle Bin, shown as a wastepaper basket, displays when *Windows* is installed. Other icons and shortcuts may be added.

- ■ *Desktop* ❻. This is the work area where you will be working on your documents and programs.

SHUT DOWN COMPUTER

Microsoft has made it easy for you to interface with the *Windows 8* features by using either keyboard shortcuts or by moving the mouse to the "hot corners" of the computer screen. Many of the keyboard shortcuts utilize the Windows key (Winkey) and another key. For example, pressing Winkey + D displays the *Windows* desktop, and Winkey + E opens *File Explorer*. The Windows key (⊞) is located to the left of the space bar.

Charms are icons that provide quick access to *Windows 8* launch areas. The five Charms are Search, Share, Start, Devices, and Settings. Point to the lower-right corner of the screen to display the Charms bar. You can also display the Charms bar by pressing Winkey + C.

Charms bar

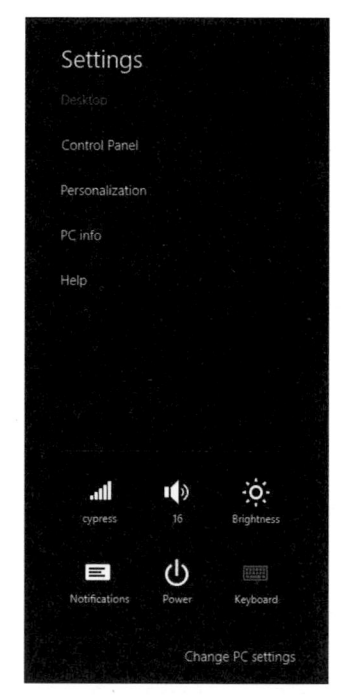

Settings options

To shut down the computer:

1. Display the Charms bar, Winkey + C.
2. Click the Settings charm to display the Settings options.
3. Click Power to display the Power options menu.
4. Click Shut down.

Sleep
Shut down
Restart

Power options

DRILL 1	START WINDOWS

1. Sign in to *Windows 8*.

2. Display the *Windows 8* Start screen.

3. Click the Weather tile; the Weather app displays full screen.

4. Click the WinKey to display the Start screen.

5. Click the Finance tile to display the Finance app. Click the right arrow in the lower-right corner of the screen to scroll through the Finance app.

6. Move the mouse to the lower-left corner of the screen; click the Start screen icon.

7. Right-click on any empty spot on the Start screen and click the All apps button.

8. Press WinKey + C to display the Charms bar.

9. Click the Settings charm.

10. Click Power, then Shut down.

WINDOWS 8 HELP

The *Windows 8 Help and Support* feature contains documentation on how to use *Windows 8*; this feature is stored on your computer. Additional links are provided that will take you to the Microsoft site for more information, if you are connected to the Internet.

The easiest way to display Windows Help and Support is to press F1 from the Desktop. The Help feature can also be access from Settings options (Charms bar/Settings/Help). To search for help, key your topic in the Search box, then click the Search button. A list of topics will display; click the link to display the information.

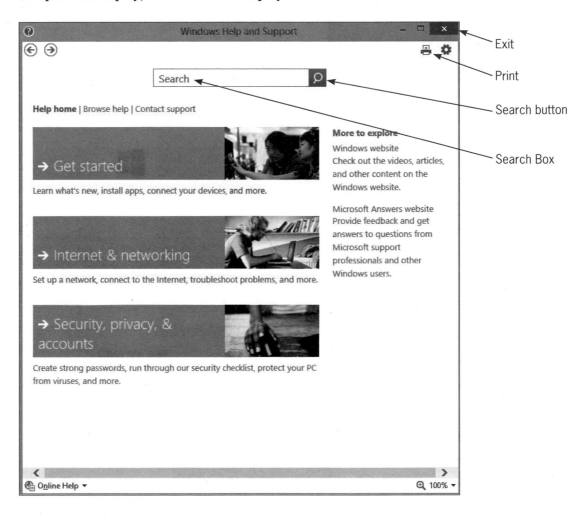

Exit

Print

Search button

Search Box

DRILL 2　　　USING WINDOWS HELP

DRILL 2 — USING WINDOWS HELP

1. Sign in to *Windows 8*. From the *Windows 8* desktop, press F1.

2. The *Windows 8* Help and Support screen displays.

3. Click Get started.

4. Click the Get to know Windows link.

5. Key **keyboard shortcuts** in the Search box.

6. Click the Search button.

7. Click the link–Mouse and Keyboard: What's new.

8. Read the information that displays. Click the Print button in the upper-right of the screen.

9. Click the exit button in the upper-right of the pane to close the Windows Help and Support screen.

File Management

FILE EXPLORER

Data is stored in files on the computer. To use the files, you need to know the name of the file and the location in which the file is saved. *Windows 8* stores related files in folders. Folders can also be stored within folders, called subfolders. *File Explorer* provides the interface for you to manage the file system. Click the File Explorer icon on the Taskbar to display the *File Explorer* window.

The left pane is the Navigation pane, which shows the drives on the computer and the files stored on each drive. If an expand icon ▷ displays to the left of the folder or drive, that means that the folder or drive contains subfolders. You can expand the list to view the subfolders by clicking the ▷ icon. Once the list is expanded, the expand icon changes to a collapse icon; clicking the collapse icon ◢ will hide the subfolders.

The Contents pane lists the contents of the folders. Click on a folder in the Navigation pane to display the contents of the folder in the Contents pane. If you want to get a preview of what a file looks like, click the View tab, then in the Panes group click Preview pane to display an additional pane that shows a preview of your file.

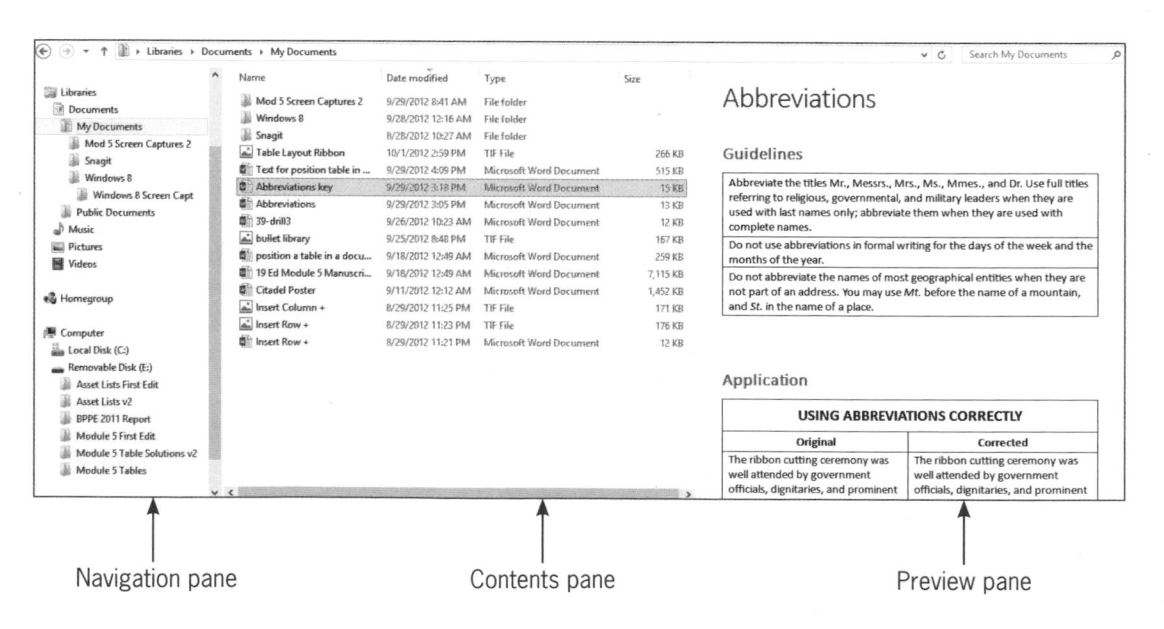

Navigation pane   Contents pane   Preview pane

When you open *File Explorer*, it displays four default libraries—Documents, Music, Pictures, and Videos. The libraries display similar types of files regardless of the drive they are stored on. The Pictures Library will list all the pictures stored on the C: drive as well as any that you may have on a USB drive or other external drives that are plugged into the computer. The Documents Library lists all the documents (*Word, Excel, PowerPoint,* etc.) that are stored on drives connected to the computer. This differs from the way the Navigation pane displays the folders, in that the Navigation pane displays according to the contents of each drive.

Documents, by default, save in the My Documents folder. To view the My Documents folder, move the mouse over Documents in the left pane; then click the expand icon. Click the expand icon to the left of the My Documents folder to display its contents.

Files can be stored in various locations or drives on the computer. To view the drives on your computer, click Computer in the Navigation pane. The drives on your computer display in the right pane. The drives are labeled with letters followed by a colon (C:, D:, E:). The hard drive, which stores the software, is usually labeled as drive (C:) If you are using a USB drive to save your files, the USB drive is often designated as drive E: or F:

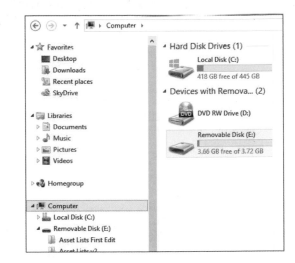

FILE ADDRESSES

The address bar, located above the Navigation and Contents pane, shows the location or address of the file. Each level of the file hierarchy is separated with a ▶ symbol; the highest level display at the left of the address bar. The ▶ symbol indicates the next lower level. The illustration below shows that the selected file, Windows 8 Manuscript, is located in the Windows 8 subfolder ❶, which is located in the My Documents folder ❷, in the Documents Library ❸.

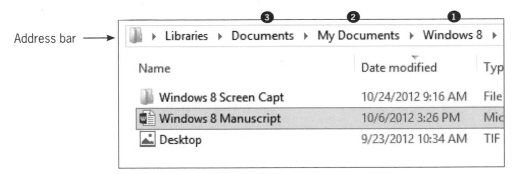

Address bar

You can move up the hierarchy by clicking on the higher level in the address bar or by clicking on a higher level in the Navigation pane. You can also display the contents of the folder by clicking on the folder name in the address bar.

WORK WITH FILES AND FOLDERS

Folders are extremely important in organizing files. You will create and manage folders and the files within them so that you can easily locate them. A folder can store files; or a folder may contain subfolders which store files. The use of folders and subfolders helps to reduce clutter so that you can find, navigate, and manage your files, folders, and disks with greater speed.

NAMING FILES

Good file organization begins with giving your folders and files names that are logical and easy to understand. A filename should be meaningful and reflect the contents of the file. Filenames can be up to 255 characters long (but in practice you won't use filenames that long). In addition, the following symbols cannot be used in a filename: \ / : * ? " , . The descriptive name is followed by a period (.), which is used to separate the descriptive name from the file extension. The file extension is three or four letters that follow the period. When renaming a file, do not delete or change file extensions as this may cause problems opening the file.

FILE EXPLORER HOME RIBBON

Commands that are commonly used are located on the Home tab. The ribbon is divided into groups, similar to that of other *Microsoft Office* products. The commands to create new folders, rename files and folders, and copy, move and delete files are all located on the Home tab.

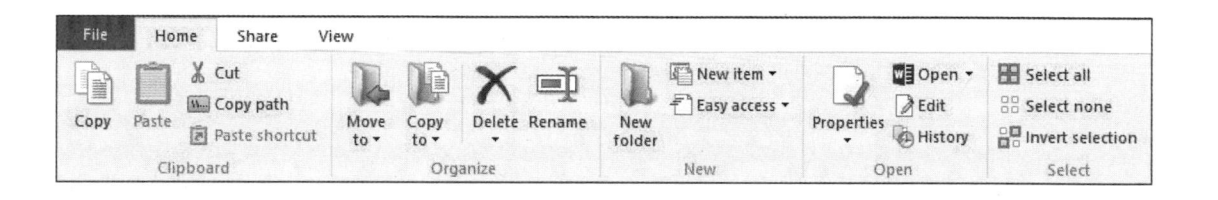

To create a file folder:
Home/New/New Folder

1. In the left pane of *File Explorer*, click the drive or folder that is to contain the new folder.
2. Follow the path to create a new folder. A yellow folder icon displays at the top of the right pane with the words *New folder* highlighted.
3. Key the new folder name and tap ENTER.

To rename a file or folder:
Home/Organize/Rename

1. Access *File Explorer* and display the contents of your removable storage drive (or the location where you have been instructed to save your document files or folders).
2. Click the file or folder icon to be renamed.
3. Click Rename on the ribbon.
4. Key the new name and tap ENTER.

COPY, MOVE, OR DELETE FILES OR FOLDERS

The names of the files need to be selected from the Contents pane in order to use the commands in the Home ribbon.

To move a file or folder to a new location, select the file and click the *Move to* command. Select a location from the drop list or click *Choose location* to display the *Move items* dialog box. Select the location the file or folder is to be moved to, then click the *Move* button.

Copy a file to leave it in its current location and make a duplicate of it in another location. To place a copy of a file or folder in a new location, select the file and click the *Copy to* command. Select a location from the drop list or click *Choose location* to display the *Copy items* dialog box. Select the location the file or folder is to be copied to, then click the *Copy* button.

To delete a file or folder, highlight the file or folder icon in the *Explorer* window and click Delete in the ribbon. When you delete a file or folder from the hard drive, it is not removed from the storage immediately. It moves to the Recycle Bin and remains there until the Recycle Bin is emptied. This gives you the opportunity to restore the file to its original location if you discover that it should not have been deleted.

SKYDRIVE APP

SkyDrive

Updates are continually made to the SkyDrive. Read your screen carefully as appearance and steps may vary over time.

Microsoft made the SkyDrive an integral part of the *Windows 8* operating system by placing the SkyDrive app on the Start screen. The SkyDrive is a service that allows you to store documents, photos, videos, and audio files on the *Microsoft* servers. A benefit of storing files on the SkyDrive is the ability to access the files from any computer or *Windows* phone. The files can be shared with family and friends. Co-workers can collaboratively work on *Microsoft Office* documents. You need to have a *Microsoft* account to access the SkyDrive.

To access the SkyDrive: *(Internet connection needed with a Microsoft account.)*

1. From the *Windows 8* Start screen, click the SkyDrive app icon.
2. Your SkyDrive Home location displays. Folders display the folder name and the number of files in the folder. Files display the file name and an icon identifying the file type. Picture files contain a preview of the picture file.
3. Click the file or folder to open it.

To upload a file to SkyDrive:

1. From the *Windows 8* Start screen, click the SkyDrive app icon.
2. Right-click any blank area to display a toolbar at the bottom of the screen.
3. Click New Folder. Key the folder name in the Create Folder dialog box.
4. Click the new folder to open it.
5. Right-click in the new folder and choose Upload.
6. Browse to select the file(s) to upload. A ✓ displays in the upper-right of each file that is selected. After all files are selected, click the *Add to SkyDrive* button.
7. The status of the upload displays in the upper-right corner of the SkyDrive screen. "Done" displays when the upload is complete.

To download a file to your computer:

1. Select the file(s) to be downloaded.
2. Click the Download button.
3. Choose the location to place the file.
4. Click the *Choose this folder* button in the lower-right; then click OK.

DRILL 3   UPLOADING A FILE TO SKYDRIVE   genevieve

1. Click the SkyDrive app on the Start screen.
2. On your SkyDrive home page, right-click and choose New Folder.
3. Name the folder **SkyDrive Assignments**.
4. Click the folder to open it. Right-click in the folder and choose Upload.
5. Navigate to the folder and select the **Genevieve** file.

6. Click the Add to SkyDrive button.
7. Click the down arrow to the right of SkyDrive Assignments; choose your SkyDrive from the list that displays.
8. Press the WinKey to return to the Start screen.
9. Log off or shut down the computer.

Digital Citizenship

OVERVIEW

One search using a popular search engine and *digital citizenship* as keywords produced over three million results. A quick survey of the list of documents indicated that digital citizenship is a popular, if not required, topic in the curricula of K-12 schools. Many of the documents focused on digital citizenship research by Dr. Mike Ribble, on the framework developed by the Partnership for 21st Century Skills, and on the International Society for Technology in Education Standards for Students. A relatively small percentage of the documents listed referred to collegiate education or business and industry.

This article focuses on effective digital citizenship from four perspectives that can affect your career.

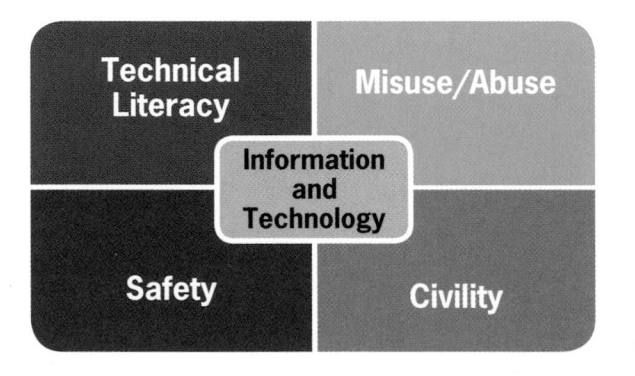

TECHNICAL LITERACY

Understanding how the Internet, social media applications, and other digital tools work enables you to use these tools creatively, responsibly, and safely. Technology is constantly evolving; things learned today can be outdated in a very short time. Therefore, continual learning is the only way to keep up with technology. Protecting your (or your company's) computer, network, and information from unauthorized access is critical. Many students and young employees who have grown up using all types of technology may be more technically savvy than their instructors or their managers. However, they often do not have the social skills and business savvy to be effective in using digital tools.

MISUSE/ABUSE

The Internet is a vast collection of information that can be accessed easily and at little or no cost. However, just because information has been posted on the Internet does not mean that it is accurate or valid.

Information Verification. Information should be analyzed carefully to determine the credibility of the writer, source of the information, accuracy of details, knowledge of the literature, and the currency of the information before relying on that information.

Plagiarism. Copyright laws protect material from unauthorized use. Request permission before using copyrighted materials. It is not acceptable to copy information from the Internet without properly documenting the source of the information and giving the writer proper credit. Software is available to check a paper and quickly determine if it has been plagiarized.

Piracy. Downloading of music, games, and movies and making copies of software without permission are illegal.

SAFETY

Privacy. Protecting private information and company proprietary information are key safety concerns. Protect your information and/or your company's information by using up-to-date antivirus software, antispyware, and firewalls.

Identity theft. Unauthorized persons may obtain information such as your Social Security number or credit card information and use it for criminal purposes. Posting private information on social networks can have serious negative consequences as shown in the following examples.

- Posting pictures of vacation sites and travel information alerted criminals that the family was away and their home was robbed.
- Posting pictures of children on the Internet and address information in other locations attracted predators to the home.
- Unprofessional information and pictures on a social network were viewed by a potential employer causing the person not to be hired. Many employers check out potential employees on social networks before hiring them.
- Negative information posted about a person's supervisor and company was viewed by company executives.

CIVILITY

Courtesy and good manners when posting information, sending emails, participating in a chat room, blogging, or posting on a social media site are always appropriate. The following tips are examples of good *netiquette*.

- Consider anything you post to be public information. Many people use technology to deliver messages that they would never send in a face-to-face situation.
- Use appropriate, non-offensive language and be sensitive to cultural issues.
- Avoid inflammatory messages and messages keyed in all capital letters.

- Be helpful to people who have less technical expertise than you do. They may have great ideas even though they are not technically savvy.
- Avoid texting and checking and sending emails, and place cell phones on vibrate during meetings and dining.

Keyboarding—Bridge to Today's Technology

WHO NEEDS A KEYBOARD WITH TODAY'S TECHNOLOGY?

This question is frequently asked and framed in many ways. Often it takes the form of: Are keyboarding skills still valid and necessary with touch, pen, and voice technology available?

The most frequent answer to the question is that everyone who needs a computer in their lives or in their jobs needs keyboarding skill. It is simply a prerequisite for effective and productive use of today's technology. Note the keywords—effective and productive use. Individuals who do not have effective touch keyboarding skills are at a significant disadvantage using today's technology. It is clear that the self-taught hunt and peck system is neither adequate nor acceptable. Voice technology, pen technology, the mouse, and touch technology have been in existence for a number of years and, for many years, have been predicted to replace keyboarding skill. Yet, market penetration for those skills in business offices is negligible. Touch technology has proliferated on mobile devices primarily for navigation. However, it cannot replace the keyboard for keying the documents, spreadsheets, or presentations are used extensively in business. The need for keyboarding skills continues to flourish, and the investment in developing keyboarding skills continues to be a wise one.

WHAT JOBS REQUIRE COMPUTERS (AND THUS KEYBOARDING SKILLS)?

A number of years ago, keyboarding skills were often thought of as clerical skills. Today, most estimates show that keyboarding skills are communication and technical skills used in more than 90 percent of all jobs. Careers that are enhanced significantly by keyboarding skills include medical, legal, business, journalism, scientific, engineering, teaching, and numerous other fields.

The casual home use with a laptop illustrated at the right would not be productive in the careers listed above. Developing excellent keyboarding techniques and skills is necessary to use computers effectively in the workplace.

© iStockphoto/Ruslan Dashinsky

The keyboard is likely to be the primary input device for computers for many years to come. Learn to use it effectively!

YOU ARE IN CHARGE!

Medical self-management is a very popular concept in the prevention, treatment, and control of diseases, such as chronic pain, diabetes, asthma, stress, high blood pressure, and many others. Patients can be trained to prevent, treat, and control many of the symptoms and problems caused by these diseases. If fact, some patients become more effective managing their disease than their medical staff. A number of health issues may be associated with the use of technology, but nobody is in a better position to prevent and manage these issues than you are. The most important concept to remember is that prevention is far more effective than curing health issues.

TECHNOLOGY HEALTH ISSUES

Many computer users are quick to blame the monitor, keyboard, and mouse for eye strain, repetitive stress injuries (RSI), cumulative trauma disorders (CTDs), and carpal tunnel syndrome (CTS). The appropriate question is: Is the technology the cause of the problems or is the real culprit the way the technology is set up and used?

Which of the three extensive computer users pictured here is least likely to experience some of the issues listed above?

The user in the center is least likely to experience some of the issues listed above for several reasons:

- He is the only one not using a laptop or treating the keyboard like a laptop. Laptops are difficult to position comfortably because the screen and keyboard are both attached. With a laptop, typically the screen is too low or the keyboard is too high.
- With the desktop computer, the screen is large and is positioned at a comfortable height and distance; the keyboard is at the correct height and the mouse is next to it.
- The user's posture, hand, and arm position are correct.
- The user on the left is likely to have difficulty reading the screen because of the distance, the upward tilt, and the glare. The "leaning back" posture with keyboard on her lap with poor hand and wrist position will likely lead to fatigue and poor results.
- The user on the right is using a laptop that is placed too far from the front edge of the table with her left arm resting on the table and laptop. She is also leaning over the table, which is higher than desired, and looking downward to see the screen.

Note the proper way to set up your work environment on the next page, and critique the pictures again.

SET UP YOUR WORK ENVIRONMENT

The setup depends on the physical size of the individual and the type of computer being used.

Laptops

Laptop and tablet computers are not designed ergonomically. They are fine for occasional use, but are not as effective for extensive computer use. Laptops used extensively are best set up with a docking station which allows the user to plug in a separate monitor and/or a separate keyboard. The laptop can then be set up in the same manner that a desktop computer is set up.

Desktop Computers

The position of the monitor, keyboard, mouse, and chair are important. A few guides to follow:

- Position the screen so that the top is at about eye level and about arm's length from the user. Avoid glare from windows if possible. Increase the size of the text and icons on the screen if necessary.
- The keyboard tray should be positioned so that it is about two inches above your thighs and your arms are parallel to the floor.
- The mouse should be positioned close to the keyboard.
- Adjust the chair to a comfortable position.

POSITION THE USER APPROPRIATELY

Correct posture and hand position are important. Moving around and frequent breaks are also important. Exercises to relax your eyes and strengthen your fingers and muscles are also helpful.

- Sit upright in the chair and face the computer; feet should be flat on the floor.
- Arms should be parallel to the floor and wrists straight.
- Position the arms close to the body.
- User position should be such that extended reaching is not necessary.

Index